CONTENTS

AUTISM SPECTRUM DISORDERS: AN UPDATE OF FEDERAL GOVERNMENT INITIATIVES AND REVOLUTIONARY NEW TREATMENT OF NEURO-DEVELOPMENTAL DISEASES

HEARING

BEFORE THE

SUBCOMMITTEE ON HUMAN RIGHTS AND WELLNESS

OF THE

COMMITTEE ON GOVERNMENT REFORM

HOUSE OF REPRESENTATIVES

ONE HUNDRED EIGHTH CONGRESS

SECOND SESSION

MAY 6, 2004

Serial No. 108–192

Printed for the use of the Committee on Government Reform

Available via the World Wide Web: http://www.gpo.gov/congress/house
http://www.house.gov/reform

U.S. GOVERNMENT PRINTING OFFICE

95–740 PDF WASHINGTON : 2004

For sale by the Superintendent of Documents, U.S. Government Printing Office
Internet: bookstore.gpo.gov Phone: toll free (866) 512–1800; DC area (202) 512–1800
Fax: (202) 512–2250 Mail: Stop SSOP, Washington, DC 20402–0001

COMMITTEE ON GOVERNMENT REFORM

TOM DAVIS, Virginia, *Chairman*

DAN BURTON, Indiana
CHRISTOPHER SHAYS, Connecticut
ILEANA ROS-LEHTINEN, Florida
JOHN M. McHUGH, New York
JOHN L. MICA, Florida
MARK E. SOUDER, Indiana
STEVEN C. LaTOURETTE, Ohio
DOUG OSE, California
RON LEWIS, Kentucky
JO ANN DAVIS, Virginia
TODD RUSSELL PLATTS, Pennsylvania
CHRIS CANNON, Utah
ADAM H. PUTNAM, Florida
EDWARD L. SCHROCK, Virginia
JOHN J. DUNCAN, Jr., Tennessee
NATHAN DEAL, Georgia
CANDICE S. MILLER, Michigan
TIM MURPHY, Pennsylvania
MICHAEL R. TURNER, Ohio
JOHN R. CARTER, Texas
MARSHA BLACKBURN, Tennessee
PATRICK J. TIBERI, Ohio
KATHERINE HARRIS, Florida

HENRY A. WAXMAN, California
TOM LANTOS, California
MAJOR R. OWENS, New York
EDOLPHUS TOWNS, New York
PAUL E. KANJORSKI, Pennsylvania
CAROLYN B. MALONEY, New York
ELIJAH E. CUMMINGS, Maryland
DENNIS J. KUCINICH, Ohio
DANNY K. DAVIS, Illinois
JOHN F. TIERNEY, Massachusetts
WM. LACY CLAY, Missouri
DIANE E. WATSON, California
STEPHEN F. LYNCH, Massachusetts
CHRIS VAN HOLLEN, Maryland
LINDA T. SANCHEZ, California
C.A. "DUTCH" RUPPERSBERGER, Maryland
ELEANOR HOLMES NORTON, District of Columbia
JIM COOPER, Tennessee

BERNARD SANDERS, Vermont (Independent)

MELISSA WOJCIAK, *Staff Director*
DAVID MARIN, *Deputy Staff Director/Communications Director*
ROB BORDEN, *Parliamentarian*
TERESA AUSTIN, *Chief Clerk*
PHIL BARNET, *Minority Chief of Staff/Chief Counsel*

SUBCOMMITTEE ON HUMAN RIGHTS AND WELLNESS

DAN BURTON, Indiana, *Chairman*

CHRIS CANNON, Utah
CHRISTOPHER SHAYS, Connecticut
ILEANA ROS-LEHTINEN, Florida

DIANE E. WATSON, California
BERNARD SANDERS, Vermont (Independent)
ELIJAH E. CUMMINGS, Maryland

EX OFFICIO

TOM DAVIS, Virginia

HENRY A. WAXMAN, California

MARK WALKER, *Chief of Staff*
MINDI WALKER, *Professional Staff Member*
DANIELLE PERRAUT, *Clerk*
RICHARD BUTCHER, *Minority Counsel*

AUTISM SPECTRUM DISORDERS: AN UPDATE OF FEDERAL GOVERNMENT INITIATIVES AND REVOLUTIONARY NEW TREATMENT OF NEURODEVELOPMENTAL DISEASES

THURSDAY, MAY 6, 2004

HOUSE OF REPRESENTATIVES,
SUBCOMMITTEE ON HUMAN RIGHTS AND WELLNESS,
COMMITTEE ON GOVERNMENT REFORM,
Washington, DC.

The subcommittee met, pursuant to notice, at 2:15 p.m., in room 2247, Rayburn House Office Building, Hon. Dan Burton (chairman of the subcommittee) presiding.

Present: Representatives Watson and Burton.

Also present: Representative Weldon.

Staff present: Mark Walker, staff director; Mindi Walker, Brian Fauls, and Dan Getz, professional staff members; Danielle Perraut, clerk; Nick Mutton, press secretary; Richard Butcher, minority counsel; and Jean Gosa, minority assistant clerk.

Mr. BURTON. Good afternoon. A quorum being present, the Subcommittee on Human Rights and Wellness will come to order.

I ask unanimous consent that all Members' and witnesses' written and opening statements be included in the record. Without objection, so ordered.

Congressman Watson, I understand, who is the ranking member of this subcommittee, will be here shortly.

I ask unanimous consent that all articles exhibits and extraneous or tabular materials referred to be included in the record; and, without objection, so ordered.

In the event of other Members attending today's hearing I ask unanimous consent that they be permitted to serve as a member of the subcommittee for the purpose of today's hearing. Without objection, so ordered.

The subcommittee is convening today to examine the advances in Federal Government initiatives, as well as new treatments that have been shown to benefit the medical condition of individuals afflicted with Autism Spectrum Disorder.

As many of us already know, the incidences of autism have become increasingly prevalent in modern-day society. Once considered a rare disease, affecting roughly 1 in 10,000 children, autism now affects 1.5 million of our Nation's children; and the problem continues to escalate.

According to a recent "Autism Alarm" released by the U.S. Department of Health and Human Services and the Centers for Disease Control and the American Academy of Pediatrics, currently, as I said, 1 out of every 6 children are diagnosed with a developmental disorder and/or behavioral problem. Even more alarming, today 1 out of every 166 children in the United States is being diagnosed with an Autism Spectrum Disorder.

This is a major health care crisis that has to be addressed by our health agencies because it's simply not going to "go away." It just gets worse and worse.

As such, the U.S. Government has rightfully begun to acknowledge the present and future public health implications of this autism epidemic by establishing an Interagency Autism Coordinating Committee. The IACC is comprised of representatives from HHS, the National Institutes of Health, the Department of Education, as well as various non-governmental organizations and parental support groups.

The IACC meets on a bi-annual basis to discuss and coordinate the various research projects with regard to autism, as well as to keep an open dialog in addressing the numerous health care and educational needs of individuals with autism.

To further address the concerns of the autism community, HHS and the Department of Education at long last sponsored the first-ever "National Autism Summit" in November 2003. Some of the best scientific and medical researchers, as well as autism activists, key Members of Congress, and a host of parental support groups initiated an open dialog on the status of research initiatives.

This summit was essential to bridging the relationship between the government, non-governmental organizations and private citizens.

To better explain the status of Federal Government autism initiatives, the subcommittee has the pleasure of hearing testimony today from the Honorable Troy Justesen, the Acting Assistant Secretary in the Office of Special Education and Rehabilitative Services at the U.S. Department of Education.

During my tenure as chairman of the full Committee on Government Reform, and as the current Chair of this subcommittee, I have convened 20 hearings on the topics of autism, vaccine safety, and the detrimental health effects of mercury-containing medical products.

We've been successful in getting mercury out of almost all children's vaccines except, I think—what—three. The problem is that, still on the shelves, are vaccines that are being given to children that contain mercury that are no longer being produced. We need to have a recall on those, but so far HHS and CDC has not chosen to do that. But we're working on them.

During these investigations, numerous scientists from around the globe have testified before the committee and have presented credible peer-reviewed research studies that indicated a direct link between the exposure of mercury, a widely known neurotoxin, and the increasing instances of autism. Because autistic individuals typically have a high concentration of mercury stored in their bodies, many doctors are concerned with how exactly they can safely remove these toxins from their patients without exposing them to greater medical risks.

One popular method to remove this poisonous metal, called chelation therapy, involves an intravenous solution that disperses and collects mercury, ultimately to be flushed out of the body. Unfortunately, because of the way in which this therapy is administered, it is not recommended for use with children, although some are doing it. Dr. Rashid Buttar has developed a groundbreaking transdermal chelator that has proven safe to use in treating pediatric patients.

Dr. Buttar is testifying before the subcommittee today to speak on his personal success and application of this groundbreaking treatment. I'm really anxious to hear what the doctor has to say about that. I think it will be great if it works as I hear it has.

Another cutting-edge medical development currently being used and tested for the use in autistic patients is Hyperbaric Oxygen Therapy. This treatment, which involves the delivery of pressurized oxygen to a patient, has been recently used to assist with the regeneration of neurons in brain-injured individuals. Dr. Paul Harch, president of the International Hyperbaric Medical Association, will discuss how the use of hyperbarics may be a viable therapy to administer to persons afflicted with an Autism Spectrum Disorder.

In addition, Dr. Ken Stoller has been invited to further supplement the testimony of Dr. Harch and discuss additional uses for hyperbaric treatments for patients afflicted with other neurodevelopmental diseases and injuries.

Finally, to gain the perspective of parents of brain-injured children, Ms. Julie Gordon, founder and director of MUMS, Mothers United for Moral Support, will be testifying today in regard to how coalitions of parents have come together and effectively lobbied for the advancement of their children's health.

As I stated before, autism is an epidemic, and I sure hope our health agencies are paying attention, because it really is, and it directly affects millions of Americans, including every single taxpayer in the United States and will for decades to come.

I am pleased to see that our Nation's health and education agencies are beginning to do their part to address this pandemic situation. I implore them to continue their fight against these devastating diseases and get mercury out of all vaccines for children and adults. We haven't mentioned people who are aging, who have neurological disorders, but there is a growing body of evidence that the mercury has affected them as well.

I'd like to thank all our witnesses for making the long trip to Washington for this most important hearing, and I look forward to hearing about the revolutionary treatments and current research that will hopefully 1 day completely eradicate these spectrum disorders.

[The prepared statement of Hon. Dan Burton follows:]

Opening Statement
Chairman Dan Burton
Subcommittee on Human Rights & Wellness
Government Reform Committee
"Autism Spectrum Disorders: An Update of Federal Government Initiatives and Revolutionary New Treatments of Neurodevelopmental Diseases"
May 6, 2004

The Subcommittee is convening today to examine the advances in Federal Government initiatives, as well as new treatments that have been shown to benefit the medical condition of individuals afflicted with an Autism Spectrum Disorder.

As many of us already know, the incidences of autism have become increasingly prevalent in modern-day society. Once considered a rare disease, effecting roughly 1 in 10,000 children, autism now affects 1.5 Million of our Nation's children, and this problem continues to escalate rapidly.

According to a recent "Autism Alarm" released by the U.S. Department of Health and Human Services (HHS), the Centers for Disease Control (CDC), and the American Academy of Pediatrics, currently 1 out of every 6 children are diagnosed with a developmental disorder and / or behavioral problem. Even more alarming, today 1 out of every 166 children in the United States is being diagnosed with an Autism Spectrum Disorder. This major healthcare crisis is clearly reaching epidemic proportions, and will not just simply "go away."

As such, the United States government has rightfully begun to acknowledge the present and future public health implications of this autism epidemic by establishing an Interagency Autism Coordinating Committee (IACC). The IACC is comprised of representatives from HHS, the National Institutes of Health, the Department of Education, as well as various non-governmental organizations and parental support groups.

The IACC meets on a bi-annual basis to discuss and coordinate the various research projects with regard to autism, as well as to keep an open dialogue in addressing the numerous healthcare and educational needs of individuals with autism.

To further address the concerns of the autism community, HHS and the Department of Education at long last sponsored the first-ever "National Autism Summit" in November 2003. Some of the best scientific and medical researchers, as well as autism activists, key Members of Congress, and a host of parental support groups initiated an open dialogue on the status of research initiatives.

This summit was essential to bridging the relationship between the government, non-governmental organizations, and private citizens.

To better explain the status of Federal Government autism initiatives, the Subcommittee has the pleasure of hearing testimony today from the Honorable Troy

Justesen (Justice – son), the Acting Assistant Secretary in the Office of Special Education and Rehabilitative Services, at the U.S. Department of Education.

During my tenure as the Chairman of the Full Committee on Government Reform, and as the current Chair of this Subcommittee, I have convened 20 hearings on the topics of Autism, vaccine safety, and the detrimental health effects of Mercury-containing medical products.

During these investigations, numerous scientists from around the globe have testified before the Committee and have presented credible peer-reviewed research studies that indicated a direct link between the exposure of Mercury, a widely known neurotoxin, and the increasing incidences of autism.

Because autistic individuals typically have a high concentration of Mercury stored in their bodies, many doctors are concerned with how exactly they can safely remove these toxins from their patients, without exposing them to greater medical risks.

One popular method to remove this poisonous metal, called chelation therapy, involves an intravenous solution that disperses and collects Mercury, ultimately to be flushed out of the body. Unfortunately, because of the way in which this therapy is administered, it is not recommended for use in children. Dr. Rashid Buttar (Rah-sheed, Boot-tar), has developed a groundbreaking transdermal chelator that has proven safe to use in treating pediatric patients. Dr. Buttar (Boot-tar) is testifying before the

Subcommittee today to speak on his personal success and application of this groundbreaking treatment.

Another cutting edge medical development currently being tested for use in autistic patients is Hyperbaric Oxygen Therapy. This treatment, which involves the delivery of pressurized oxygen to a patient, has been recently used to assist with the regeneration of neurons in brain-injured individuals. Dr. Paul Harch, President of the International Hyperbaric Medical Association, will discuss how the use of hyperbarics may be a viable therapy to administer to persons afflicted with an autism spectrum disorder.

In addition, Dr. Ken Stoller (Stole-er), has been invited to further supplement the testimony of Dr. Harch and discuss additional uses for hyperbaric treatments for patients afflicted with other neurodevelopmental diseases and injuries.

Finally, to gain the perspective of parents of brain-injured children, Ms. Julie Gordon, Founder and Director of MUMS (Mothers United for Moral Support), will be testifying today in regard to how coalitions of parents have come together and effectively lobbied for the advancement of their children's health.

As I stated before, autism is an epidemic that directly affects millions of Americans, including every single taxpayer in the United States. I am pleased to see that our Nation's health and education agencies are beginning to do their part to address this

pandemic situation, and I implore them to continue their fight against these devastating diseases.

I would like to thank all of our witnesses for making the long trip to Washington for this most important hearing, and I look forward to hearing about the revolutionary treatments and current research that will hopefully one day completely eradicate these spectrum disorders.

Mr. BURTON. Since Ms. Watson is not yet here, we'll go ahead and have our first panel start. That is the Honorable Troy Justesen. He is the Assistant Secretary, Acting, in the Office of Special Education and Rehabilitative Services for the Department of Education.

[Witness sworn.]

Mr. BURTON. Do you have an opening statement, sir?

Mr. JUSTESEN. I do. I will try to make it quick so you have the opportunity to hear from the more important people here, which are the parents.

First of all——

Mr. BURTON. I think what you have to say is important, too; and I have a couple questions for you.

STATEMENT OF TROY JUSTESEN, ACTING ASSISTANT SECRETARY, OFFICE OF SPECIAL EDUCATION AND REHABILITATIVE SERVICES, DEPARTMENT OF EDUCATION

Mr. JUSTESEN. OK, sir.

Thank you for the opportunity to discuss our initiatives for children with autism and Autism Spectrum Disorders [ASD], and our work at the Department of Education.

As you know, Mr. Chairman, the Individuals with Disabilities Education Act provides educational services for children with disabilities, including children with ASD, throughout the Nation's schools. Today, more than 6.9 million children with disabilities are receiving special education and related services, and that number continues to grow. As States reported in 1999 through 2002, a 1.6 percent annual increase in the number of children with disabilities receiving special education and related services. During that same time, the number of children with autism receiving special education and related services increased to an average annual rate of at least 22 percent.

We acknowledge the importance of these numbers and are focused on identifying and implementing effective, evidence-based practices for children with ASD.

This year, the Department of Education is investing $8.6 million in our discretionary funds for projects that address the needs of children with ASD. These investments fund a total of 51 projects, 31 of which focus solely on ASD, 21 of which are designed to improve services and prepare personnel to meet the needs of children with ASD as part of a larger group of children with low-incidence disabilities.

I am pleased to provide to you a highlight of some of our efforts and our investments at the Department.

In order to prepare highly qualified and trained educators to work effectively with children with ASD, we have invested in the Professional Development in Autism Center. This national research and training center is receiving $5 million over 5 years to increase the capacity of schools, families and communities to meet the needs of students with ASD. This center provides intensive hands-on training to teams of educators. It also disseminates useful information and is having a national impact through a consortium of six States across the country that includes Washington, Florida, and

Maryland. We also invest in programs that specifically address the needs of teachers and related services personnel.

Under Secretary Paige's direction, we are also making investments in research projects in Tennessee and Florida, focusing on early indicators of autism in the second and third years of life. Through these projects researchers are now accurately distinguishing some children with autism from typically developing children as early as 12 months of age. This is especially significant based on research that shows that early and accurate diagnosis and early intervention results in better outcomes for children with ASD.

Further, we continue to support model demonstration programs that develop and implement successful practices for working with children with ASD and their families. For example, the Seattle public school system has adopted an OSERS, which is the Department of Education's funded program, that blends several evidence-based practices and approaches to meet the needs of children with ASD, their families, and the educators that work with these children. The children who participate in this program have made tremendous gains across all of the domains of measurement. At this point, 418 children completed the program, and of these 58 percent of these children entered inclusive elementary programs.

With the Department's support, the project trains early education providers, teachers and family members across the State of Washington and in more than 20 other States. This project now includes a successful outreach training component designed to help educators implement and evaluate school-based programs.

The Department remains committed to providing support for families through a variety of projects. For example, we have a project in Boston that addresses parental involvement in public schools. This project promotes parental involvement in each of their child's educational programs and to increase the abilities of these parents to sustain involvement in their child's lives through their educational experiences. This project is particularly important to families of children with autism because in many cases their challenges are lifelong.

We recognize the need to work with medical research and practice communities and with other Federal agencies. To accomplish this, the Department of Education, as you mentioned earlier, actively participates in the Interagency Autism Coordinating Committee, which is chaired by the National Institute on Mental Health.

In closing, I want to emphasize to you, Mr. Chairman, and other members of the committee, that Secretary Paige and I recognize the vitally important work that needs to be done to meet the needs of children with ASD and their families and the educators who work with these children. We believe that the Individuals with Disabilities Education Act plays a critical role in supporting States, local districts, and parents in providing evidence-based practices for children with Autism Spectrum Disorders and their families and their families' friends. We remain committed to ensuring that all children are full participants in their homes, in their schools, and ultimately in their communities.

I'd like to thank you for letting me come today and offer these comments, Mr. Chairman. I'm pleased to answer any questions you may have.

[The prepared statement of Mr. Justesen follows:]

Department of Education
Statement by Troy R. Justesen, Ed.D.
Acting Deputy Assistant Secretary
Office of Special Education and Rehabilitative Services
on
Autism Spectrum Disorders: An Update of Federal Government Initiatives and Revolutionary New Treatment of Neurodevelopmental Diseases
May 6, 2004

Mr. Chairman and Members of the Subcommittee:

Good afternoon, I am Troy Justesen, the Acting Deputy Assistant Secretary for Special Education and Rehabilitative Services at the Department of Education. Thank you for the opportunity to provide an update on the Department of Education's initiatives for children with Autism Spectrum Disorders (ASD) served under the Individuals with Disabilities Education Act (IDEA).

Over the past 28 years, the IDEA has been successful in ensuring that children with disabilities have access to a free appropriate public education. Prior to the passage of the IDEA, only one in five students had access to appropriate special education services in the public schools. More than 1 million children with disabilities were excluded from the public education system and another 3.5 million children with disabilities did not receive appropriate services. Today, more than 6.9 million children with disabilities are provided early intervention and special education services.

States reported a 1.6% annual increase from 1999-2002 in the number of children with disabilities ages 6 through 21 receiving special education and related services. The number of children with autism, ages 6 through 21, receiving special education and related services increased at an average annual rate of 22% during the same time period. It is evident to school personnel that the number of children seeking services for autism spectrum disorders has greatly increased. Epidemiologists are investigating whether the numbers reflect more inclusive diagnostic criteria or, in fact, constitute a true increase in the incidence of autism spectrum disorders (ASD) in children.

The Office of Special Education Programs (OSEP) within the Office of Special Education and Rehabilitative Services (OSERS) administers the Individuals with Disabilities Education Act (IDEA). OSEP is committed to furthering effective evidence-based practices for children with ASD through research, model demonstration, outreach, technical assistance, and personnel training projects funded by IDEA, Part D discretionary investments. OSEP has invested $8.6 million of discretionary funding in fiscal year 2004 for projects that addressed the needs of children and youth with autism spectrum disorders. These investments fund a total of 51 projects, 30 of which focus solely on autism spectrum disorders and 21 of which are designed to improve services and prepare personnel to meet the needs of children with ASD as part of a larger group of children with other low-incidence disabilities.

One of the most pressing challenges for school systems in educating children with autism spectrum disorders is keeping up with the increase in highly skilled personnel needed to provide appropriate services. Some of the instructional strategies that are effective for children with ASD are relatively complex and demand sufficient practice to achieve success. We have continued to focus on meeting this need since it was first highlighted in the National Academy of Sciences Report, *Educating Children with Autism*, commissioned by OSEP in 2001.

OSEP continues to make a number of investments that are intended to prepare competent, highly trained personnel to work effectively with children with ASD in natural environments, family-focused settings, schools, and communities. For example, the Professional Development in Autism (PDA) Center is a five-year, $5 million nationa research and training center that is designed to increase the capacity of local school districts, families, and communities to meet the needs of students with ASD. The PDA Center will have a national impact through a consortium of six sites across the country: The University of Washington, the University of Kansas, the University of Colorado at Denver, the University of South Florida, the Oakstone Academy in Ohio, and the Maryland Coalition for Inclusive Education. The center provides intensive, hands-on training to teams of educators. In addition to training, the PDA center will also develop and disseminate useful materials, such as instructional procedures, activity ideas, and family/child support plans for children with ASD.

OSEP is currently funding projects that specifically address the personnel-preparation needs of teachers and related service providers who will work with children with ASD and their families. These projects target various areas including early intervention, speech and language pathology, and the development of interdisciplinary personnel. OSEP also funds additional personnel-preparation projects that involve training personnel to work with children who have autism spectrum disorders among other low-incidence disabilities.

OSEP continues to assume a leadership role in identifying and disseminating effective interventions that improve outcomes for children with ASD and their families. Initiatives are under way to develop and support promising practices in identification, assessment, and interventions. For example, the average age of diagnosis for children with ASD in the United States is 3 to 4 years of age; although most families initially express concern to their pediatricians by the time their child is 18 months old.

Through OSEP-funded research projects, *Early Identification of Children with Autism Spectrum Disorders* at Vanderbilt University and *First Words* at the University of Florida, researchers have succeeded in accurately distinguishing some children with autism from children with typical development and children with other developmental delays beginning as early as 12 months of age. Early and accurate diagnosis enables very young children with autism spectrum disorders to reap the benefits of earlier intervention, using a range of behavioral and naturalistic approaches. Research indicates that intervention provided to a child before the age of three and a half has a much greater impact than that after age five. Although there have been significant advances in genetic and biomedical research on ASD, there is currently no reliable biological marker for either autism or ASD. Therefore, screening and diagnosis for ASD must be based on behavioral features.

OSEP-funded model demonstration programs have developed and implemented successful practices for working with children with ASD and their families. For example, the Seattle Public School System has adopted a program that blends several approaches to meet the needs of children, families, and school personnel, including an OSEP-funded model approach developed at the University of Washington Experimental Education

Unit. This model approach incorporates developmentally appropriate treatments, including extended instructional time, family support, transition support, and collaborative, coordinated services, within an inclusive early childhood experience to yield improved outcomes for young children with autism and their families. Other successful model demonstration projects are being replicated in multiple states. For example, the *LEAP Learning Experiences* outreach project at the University of Colorado at Denver is being replicated in three states. This program provides training to early intervention staff working with children with ASD. *Project DATA,* developed at the University of Washington, has expanded to an outreach training project designed to help district personnel implement and evaluate school-based programs for young children with autism.

Addressing the often-complex needs of children with ASD is a salient research and practice issue. Autism Spectrum Disorders are characterized as a triad of disabilities that include communication, social interaction, and restrictive or repetitive behaviors. In order to address the need for research on communication skills for children with autism, Northeastern University is examining whether speech output from synthetic or digitized speech-generating devices will result in more efficient requesting and vocalizations among students with autism.

Current intervention and practice projects related to ASD include the *Early Social Interaction Project* at Florida State University, which is designed to teach very young children with ASD in natural environments, and a project at the University of Florida through which an evidence based curriculum is being developed to facilitate social success of young children with autism in natural settings.

Autism spectrum disorders pose unique and difficult challenges for families. The Department is committed to addressing these challenges and supporting families through a variety of projects. For example, a project through the University of Massachusetts at Boston addresses parent involvement in public school programs, while *FAMILY LINKS* at Case Western Reserve University uses a developmental, relationship-focused intervention for children with autism. *Project TASK* in Ohio addresses the needs of children with autism as they move to school from kindergarten.

To maximize the impact of the Department's initiatives on behalf of children with autism spectrum disorders, OSEP maintains ongoing partnerships with the medical research and practice communities and with other Federal agencies. The Interagency Autism Coordinating Committee (IACC), chaired by the National Institute of Mental Health, is one example of a formal Federal agency partnership.

The Department has participated actively as a member of the IACC since its first meeting in 2001. Through the work of this Committee, the Department is able to exchange information on autism initiatives among government agencies and with advocacy and other groups focused on autism, and improve the coordination of autism-related activities.

In a joint effort, the IACC, with the Department of Health and Human Services and the Department of Education, hosted the Autism Summit Conference in November 2003. This conference complemented the activities of the several government organizations that have been members of the IACC since its inception. At the conference, IACC members discussed a ten-year plan for implementation by Federal agencies to address research goals and activities focused on enhancing understanding of the causes and best treatment options for autism.

OSEP funds technical assistance centers and projects to assist states in implementing effective evidence-based practices to support children served under the IDEA. Centers, such as the National Early Childhood Technical Assistance Center in North Carolina and the National Center on Dispute Resolution in Oregon, continue to focus resources on ensuring that information on effective practices in ASD and other disabilities are made available to State Educational Agencies.

OSEP-funded Parent Training and Information Projects and Community Parent Resource Centers in 50 states and in many communities provide information and advocacy for families of children with disabilities, including autism, as they address their child's complex developmental and educational needs. Access for all families of children with autism spectrum disorders, regardless of family resources, to programs based on effective, evidence-based, well-implemented, models remains the highest priority.

In closing, students with autism spectrum disorders present unique challenges to families and schools. The IDEA Part D programs play a critical role in supporting states and local districts in providing evidence-based practices for children with disabilities and their families, including those with autism spectrum disorders, to help ensure that no child is left behind.

That concludes my prepared remarks. I will be happy to answer any questions.

Mr. BURTON. First of all, give my regards to Secretary Paige. I think he is doing an outstanding job. He's been one of the secretaries in the President's Cabinet that has always been very cooperative with the Congress, and I appreciate that.

Ms. Watson, do you have an opening statement?

Ms. WATSON. I want to thank you, Mr. Chairman.

Previously, autism was considered a rare disease, affecting roughly 1 in 10,000 children; and, according to the latest estimates, autism rates in the United States indicate that 1 in every 500 children are affected by the disorder. The rising prevalence of autism is disconcerting.

Mr. Chairman, I understand the anguish and confusion that Autism Spectrum Disorders can cause, and I am pleased to acknowledge that the U.S. Government has begun to look at the public health implications of Autism Spectrum Disorder by establishing an Interagency Autism Coordinating Committee. To address the concerns of the autism community, the U.S. Health and Human Services and the Department of Education sponsored the inaugural National Autism Summit in November 2003.

In addition, I commend the Chair for the autism focus of the Human Rights and Wellness Subcommittee. The American public should be informed to the best of our ability, and our Chair is doing that.

I would also like to thank the Honorable Troy Justesen from the Department of Education for your testimony today, and we appreciate it so much.

In my home State of California, the number of children diagnosed with autism has increased dramatically since the late 1980's. Autism is now more prevalent than childhood cancer, diabetes and Down's syndrome. If the increase in autism caseload numbers continue, in approximately 4 years the number of people with autism in the California Development Services system will equal each population of people with cerebral palsy and epilepsy that are in the system.

As a State Senator and Chair of the Health and Human Services Committee in California, I authored legislation to create a center in which research could be initiated on neurodevelopmental disorders. The University of California at Davis MIND Institute offers hope in unraveling the mystery that has long surrounded autism and Autism Spectrum Disorders, fragile X syndrome, and other developmental disorders.

The MIND Institute brings together diverse groups, parents, educators, physicians, and scientists, using an integrated, comprehensive approach in treating and finding cures for these neurodevelopmental disorders. Key research under way at the MIND Institute includes identifying the similarities and differences among children with autism, understanding the causes, working toward prevention, creating and providing the best treatment.

Mr. Chairman, it's important to encourage innovative wholistic approaches for treatment of the affected individuals; and I look forward to the presentation on the transdermal chelation process that is utilized by Dr. Rashid Buttar. Dr. Buttar and a growing number of health and science professionals postulate that heavy metal toxicity is at the root of several disorders such as Alzheimer's and autism.

Unfortunately, chelating agents are administered through intravenous drip. HIV—excuse me, IVs—and there is no Freudian slip there; it's just a mistake—IVs are not recommended for repeated use in children. A transdermal application of a chelator is a groundbreaking treatment modality in that children can benefit and participate.

It is a special treat to have Abid Buttar with us today. As a precocious 5-year-old, after treatment—and you can just wave your hand—Abid is a precocious 5-year old that, after treatment, can now verbalize his thoughts and play chess on his Scooby-Doo chessboard, as opposed to losing the ability to speak at 18 months.

I am pleased to announce that the chairman and I have nominated Dr. Buttar to the National Institute of Health for consideration of the Director's Pioneer Award. The award provides a stipend for research in areas that are not funded by main stream sources.

I also look forward to testimony from Dr. Harch, president of the International Hyperbaric Medical Association, and also Dr. Stoller. Hyperbaric oxygen therapy is a cutting-edge natural treatment and natural science that has shown promising results for patients afflicted with neurodevelopment diseases. Pressurized oxygen has also been used to explore the possibility of neuron regeneration in brain injured individuals.

So I see a very exciting future, Mr. Chairman. In this regard I think we have a lot to look forward to and thank you very much. I yield back my time.

Mr. BURTON. Thank you, Ms. Watson.

[The prepared statement of Hon. Diane E. Watson follows:]

Government Reform Subcommittee
Human Rights and Wellness
"Autism Spectrum Disorders: An Update of Federal Government Initiatives and Revolutionary New Treatments of Neurodevelopmental Diseases"
Opening Remarks
May 6, 2004
2154 RHOB – 2:00 P. M.

Congresswoman Diane E. Watson

Thank You Mr. Chairman. Previously, autism was considered a rare disease, affecting roughly 1 in 10,000 children. According to the latest estimates, autism rates in the United States indicate that 1 in every 500 children are afflicted by the disorder. The rising prevalence of autism is disconcerting.

Mr. Chairman, I understand the anguish and confusion that autism spectrum disorders can cause. I am pleased to acknowledge that the United States Government has begun to look at the public health implications of autism spectrum disorder by establishing an Interagency Autism Coordinating Committee. To address the concerns of the autism community, the United States Health and Human Services and the Department of Education sponsored the inaugural "National Autism Summit" in November 2003. In addition, I commend the chair for the autism focus of the Human Rights and Wellness Subcommittee. The American public should be informed to the best of our ability.

I would also like to thank the Honorable Troy Justesen, from the Department of Education, for testifying today.

In my home state of California, the number of children diagnosed with autism has increased dramatically since the late 1980's. Autism is now more prevalent than childhood cancer, diabetes and Down's syndrome. If the increase in autism caseload numbers continues, in approximately four years, the number of people with autism in the California Developmental Services system will equal each population of people with cerebral palsy and epilepsy in the system.

As a State Senator, and Chair of the Health and Human Services Committee, I authored legislation to create a center in which research

could be initiated on nureodevelopmental disorders. The University of California at Davis M.I.N.D. Institute offers hope in unraveling the mystery that has long surrounded autism and autism spectrum disorders, fragile X syndrome, and other developmental disorders.

The M.I.N.D. Institute brings together diverse groups - parents, educators, physicians and scientists, using an integrated, comprehensive approach in treating and finding cures for these neurodevelopmental disorders.

Key research under way at the M.I.N.D. Institute includes:

- **Identifying the similarities and differences among children with autism**

- **Understanding the causes**
- **Working towards prevention**
- **Creating and providing the best treatments**

Mr. Chairman, it is important to encourage innovative holistic approaches for treatment of afflicted individuals. I look forward to the presentation on the transdermal chelation (key-lay-shon) process that is utilized by Dr. Rashid Buttar. Dr. Buttar, and a growing number of health and science professionals, postulate that heavy metal toxicity is at the root of several disorders such as Alzheimer's and Autism.

Unfortunately, chelating agents are administered through intravenous drip.

IV's are not recommended for repeated use in children. A transdermal application of a chelator is a groundbreaking treatment modality in that children can benefit and participate.

It is a special treat to have Abi Buttar with us today. Abi is a precocious 5 year old that, after treatment, can now verbalize his thoughts and play chess on his Scooby-Doo chessboard, as opposed to loosing the ability to speak at 18 months old. I am pleased to announce that the Chairman and I have nominated Dr. Buttar to the National Institute of Health for consideration of the Director's Pioneer Award. The award provides a stipend for research in areas that are not funded by mainstream sources.

I also look forward to testimony from Dr. Harch, President of the International Hyperbaric Medical Association, and Dr. Stoller. Hyperbaric Oxygen Therapy is a cutting edge natural treatment that has shown promising results for patients afflicted with neurodevelopmental diseases. Pressurized oxygen has also been used to explore the possibility of neuron regeneration in brain-injured individuals.

Mr. Chairman, thank you, and I yield back my time.

Mr. BURTON. I just have a couple of questions for you, Mr. Secretary. Can you give us a little of the details on this 10-year plan in regard to autism that was established after the 2003 Autism Summit?

Mr. JUSTESEN. Well, I can give you a little bit of details. We can certainly provide the committee with a clear explanation because we have a chart that was developed principally by the leadership of HHS in which we developed short-term, mid-term, and long-term goals for achieving some of the research questions that remain to be answered and beyond the core medical research questions that we still need to answer how we can better educate children who have been identified as having ASD. We have that chart that is very detailed and how we are working chiefly between the Departments of Education and Health and Human Services on those initiatives.

We have begun—that work has just begun, because the conference was held, as you know, in late fall of last year; and our committee is meeting again in June. The Interagency Coordinating Committee meets again in June. We plan to meet at least twice a year as a group, as a full Federal committee, and between those core major committees to have interagency smaller subcommittees.

Mr. BURTON. If you could send us not only this chart you're talking about but any details on the timetable.

Mr. JUSTESEN. The chart outlines very clearly. We'll make sure your staff has my copy.

Mr. BURTON. We'll submit that for the record.

The other thing I'd like to ask you is, my grandson was in a special education program in Noblesville, IN, which is just north of Indianapolis. When he first was put into the program so he could get speech therapy and the sorts of things that you need when you have autism, his doctor prescribed I think three sessions a week, and they said they would only give him one a week.

And I know that many patients around the country have the same kind of problem. Their child needs continual teaching to try to overcome the handicaps that they might have. What does the Department of Education do or plan to do where the educational system says, OK, we can do this once a week, for instance—this is just an example—and the doctor says, hey, you should be doing it three times a week in order to get his speech up to where it should be?

Mr. JUSTESEN. Well, that's a very good question. That's a very complex question to answer.

Let me take a step back. As you know, your grandson has what is called an Individualized Education Program [IEP], in which your grandchild's parents, regular and special educators and other qualified experts are members of a team that evaluate the special education and related services as well as regular educational needs for your grandson.

Mr. BURTON. I'm not just talking about him. I'm talking about all kids.

Mr. JUSTESEN. This is an IEP. The membership is a requirement under the IDEA. That team together makes a determination about the individualized services that child, regardless of the child's disability, needs in order to benefit from special education and regular education.

Mr. BURTON. Pardon me for interrupting—in this particular case, I don't think it was just the doctor alone. And I know other parents have probably experienced this. It was the team, IE, the group you're talking about, that said that he needed to have this kind of continual help; and the school said because of the financial resources that they had that they were not able to provide sessions three times a week.

And the parents are really perplexed when they have a child that's damaged and they get one recommendation and then the educational system says that they can't adhere to that recommendation. What, if anything, is the Department of Education doing to try to accommodate these parents?

Mr. JUSTESEN. Well, the Department of Ed has oversight responsibility for both State and local school districts and their obligations to effectively implement the IDEA which, among other things, requires the appropriate implementation of what is clearly stipulated in each child's IEP. If that is not fully implemented, then there are concerns of which the local school district would be the first area of recourse for the parents and then the State. We have a monitoring function at the Federal level of each State's implementation of the IDEA; and Indiana is, of course, a State that we would monitor for compliance.

It is commonly misunderstood at times about what is and is not a requirement with respect to each individual child. If it's in a child's IEP and it has been agreed by the child's IEP team, those are services that must be provided in accordance with what is clearly written in that child's IEP. We ultimately at the Federal level have the responsibility to ensure that basic right for each child is ultimately respected.

Mr. BURTON. That's good information, because I think not only the people here in the audience but I'm sure parents around the country would like to know what the appeal process is. So they go first to their legal school board and say they're not complying and then if that doesn't work they go to the State superintendent of education.

Mr. JUSTESEN. Well, yes—if I may, the first stage of course should be a discussion with the IEP team; and then also——

Mr. BURTON. Don't worry about that. That's just the President calling all of us.

Mr. JUSTESEN. I'm glad he is calling you and not me.

Mr. BURTON. We have a series of votes coming up.

Mr. JUSTESEN. But the opportunity to mediate disputes among members of the IEP team is very important, and we don't find—and it isn't a good practice to resort to litigation or confrontation or due process as we call it under the statute to protect the individual rights and opportunities for the patients.

Mr. BURTON. I understand. I will yield to Ms. Watson. I understand. And that's—in our case, we talked to the teachers and the people in the school and then we went—what was necessary to make sure the law was followed.

But I think, for everybody else, that is extremely important to know there is an appeals process and not only do you talk to the school and the teachers but you also go to the local school board and, if necessary, to the State; and then usually you can get that problem resolved.

Ms. Watson.

Ms. WATSON. I just want to followup, Mr. Chairman. I just—one question. It seems like you are defining your mission. Is the way the coordinating committee is constituted going to have enough influence to affect programs?

Mr. JUSTESEN. Well, Dr. Watson—I'm sorry, I'm an academic doctor, Congresswoman.

Ms. WATSON. That's all right. You can call me Dr. Watson in this environment.

Mr. JUSTESEN. I think it's important for us to have the opportunity as an interagency coordinating council—which isn't something that the Federal Government, as you well know, is accustomed to working beyond from one agency to another in an interagency perspective. We have an opportunity to build on our very first meeting that we held last fall and to begin working in and understanding that these are more than just basic questions that are relevant to only one Federal agency, that the concerns of children with autism and autistic spectrum disorders, pervasive developmental disorders, and other disorders along this spectrum, that it is the responsibility of the entire Federal Government and those agencies that specialize in providing support for their children and for educators and their parents.

So, yes, give us——

Ms. WATSON. I'm sorry to cut you off. We're going to have to go to the floor.

But is this part of 97–142, that funding comes underneath that? Because I know there was mention of the Leave No Child Behind, which is, at this point, unfunded mandate. So is there a pot of money at the States?

Mr. JUSTESEN. Are there funds especially for the interagency coordinating council? I'm sorry.

Ms. WATSON. The umbrella for autism.

Mr. JUSTESEN. Oh, yes, the IDEA is an investment in more than 6.8 million children with disabilities. That includes children with autism.

Ms. WATSON. So we can move forward with your agenda.

Mr. JUSTESEN. An investment in No Child Left Behind, which is an elementary and secondary—is also an investment in children with disabilities.

Ms. WATSON. I want to thank you so much for stating that, and I would hope that you would keep a strong commitment. We worked on it for years, as I mentioned, in California. We're very, very involved; and I know the Chair is. We're working together to see that the services are delivered so we can have more young children we can be proud of who have already made this step into a normal behavior, normal speech; and I commend you for your efforts as I run out the door to vote.

Mr. JUSTESEN. By the way, we have four research initiatives in California.

Ms. WATSON. Great.

Mr. BURTON. Secretary Justesen, we really appreciate your testimony today. Once again, give our regards to the Secretary.

Ladies and gentlemen, we have three votes on the floor; and that means that we'll probably be at least 30, 35 minutes before we get back here. I don't want you all to just sit there. So if you want to get up and move around or get a Coke or something, go ahead and do that. But we'll be back here probably about a quarter after or 20 after 3.

So we stand in recess at the fall of the gavel.

[Recess.]

Mr. BURTON. The committee will reconvene.

The second panel is Dr. Rashid Buttar. He is the creator of a transdermal chelator; and he is from Cornelius, NC.

Would you come forward, Doctor?

We also have Dr. Paul Harch, the president of the International Hyperbaric Medical Association; Dr. Ken Stoller, he is a doctor from Santa Fe, NM; and Ms. Julie Gordon, she's the founder and director of MUMS, Mothers United for Moral Support.

Would you all stand and be sworn.

[Witnesses sworn.]

Mr. BURTON. I'm sorry for the delay. As I told you, we were going to be tied up with some votes. If you could, try to keep your opening statements to around 5 minutes. I would really appreciate it, because we want to get to questions as quickly as possible.

Let me start with Mr. Buttar, since he was the first one we named here. Dr. Buttar.

STATEMENTS OF RASHID BUTTAR, DO, CREATOR OF A TRANSDERMAL CHELATOR, CORNELIUS, NC; PAUL HARCH, M.D., PRESIDENT, INTERNATIONAL HYPERBARIC MEDICAL ASSOCIATION; KEN STOLLER, M.D., SANTA FE, NM; AND JULIE GORDON, FOUNDER AND DIRECTOR, MUMS—MOTHERS UNITED FOR MORAL SUPPORT, ACCOMPANIED BY SHANNON KENTIZ OF WISCONSIN

Dr. BUTTAR. First, Congressman Burton, I want to thank you on behalf of the millions of people that appreciate what you have been doing. I just wanted to start off by saying that we all appreciate your battles that you have fought on our behalf for years and years and years.

You have a presentation in front of you, I believe, a power point presentation.

Mr. BURTON. Let me get that real quick here. Oh, yes. OK. I have it.

Go ahead, Doctor.

Dr. BUTTAR. I'd like to start off by first pointing out that the overwhelming evidence of mercury and chronic disease has been reviewed and yet still it's considered to be a controversy.

On the second slide there, you'll see I did a search under TOXLINE under the ATSDR division of CDC.

We did a search under mercury and a number of different chronic diseases; and what's interesting is that, although in the medical literature there's very little evidence of mercury associated with chronic diseases, the amount of references that I found with mercury and cardiovascular disease, as you can see from that slide, amounts to 358 studies.

Why is that important? I'll explain that in just a second.

If you look at slide No. 3, mercury and cancer, there is over 643 references in the didactic literature that explains the relationship between mercury and cancer. Then when you go to the neurodegenerative area, mercury in the brain, over 1,445 references regarding the relationship between mercury and neurodegeneration; and yet for some reason still it's considered to be a controversy. There is no controversy, as you know, Mr. Congressman.

Where do we get mercury? We get mercury from everywhere: combustion of fossil fuels, from amalgams, from the water we drink—of course, we know about the Thimerosal issue with the vaccines—from the food we eat. So if it's idea to be so devastating—and why is it considered so devastating? If you look at the statistics from the World Health Organization that was published in 1998, the association between—well, they basically stated that 80 percent of all causes of death, which is not only disease processes but homicide, suicide, accidents, etc., 8 out of all 10 causes of death are either cardiovascular or cancer. And mercury is directly related to those two. When you take into consideration the neurodegenerative diseases, you're looking at 95 percent causes of all death could be attributable or contributed to by mercury. So this is a very significant problem, beyond autism and the rest of the spectrum that we're going to discuss today.

Now looking at where mercury goes in the body it goes essentially everywhere, which you see on slide No. 8. But what I am here to discuss with you today that you have asked me to come and discuss is how do we get the stuff out.

On slide No. 10 you'll see a patient, a 44-year-old female, and this is how we typically expect mercury to show up. You'll notice in the middle of the page at the bottom the challenging agent here was DMPS, a chemical that is used selectively from mercury and arsenic; and you'll notice that woman's mercury level was 65 micrograms per gram creatinin. Normal is considered anything less than 3.

And as we treat this woman you see that each time we test her, her mercury comes down. It's down to 29 in slide No. 11. Down to 21 in slide No. 12. Then, in slide No. 13, it jumps up to 41, but that's because we added a substance of glutathione that potentiates the effect of the MPS and helps to pull out more. Then we see the continuation of the mercury levels dropping. It drops down to 21 again when adding the glutathione and DMPS.

The point of these slides is to show that when we measure mercury in these tests we are not just measuring the amount of mercury in the body, because there is no way to accurately do that. The only way to accurately do that is by multiple-site biopsy which, of course, is not conducive to life. The only method that we are using right now to determine mercury issues is by the amount of mercury that we're pulling out. So these tests only show us what is being pulled out, not what's in the body. So we rely upon these types of tests to determine if mercury is an issue or not.

In the autistic population as well as in the Alzheimer's population, we have a phenomena called an impaired detoxification pathway, meaning that they cannot get rid of the mercury. So when we test them, they don't show it, even using our techniques of—the advanced techniques of using IV therapies to challenge the body.

So if you look on slide No. 16 we now have a case of a 34-year-old woman with significant medical problems, including hormonal disruptions, cardiac disrhythmia. She had ataxia, she couldn't walk straight, she had a problem speaking, she had milk coming out of her breasts, and she was 34 years old. She was suicidal. She had 16 doctors in 5 years before she came to see me. I told her this was mercury. She said she had been checked for mercury. I told her that did not count. We had to do an IV treatment. She said she had this done exactly the way I do it.

I called her doctor, and her doctor was one of my students who had come to one of my workshops and was following my protocol. We repeated this test. As you can see, she had no mercury there. This is after two tests, 2.8 micrograms per gram creatinin, no mercury. We have tested her twice over a period of year and a half.

Then she asked me the question that basically changed how I practice medicine and leads me to be in front of you today. She asked me, if I was your sister, how would you treat me? And I'd like to think I treat all my patients like I do my family members, but I told her, if you were my sister, I would not rely upon this test result. I would start treating you. She asked me to start treating her.

You will see on the slide No. 17 after 20 IV treatments her mercury level is now 9.4. It is increased exponentially. You will notice her arsenic level went from a mere 13 up to 260. This is exemplifying the point that we're here for today with autism. These patients cannot eliminate mercury.

On slide 18, you see continuation of the same patient. Her mercury level is now 19, and yet she's getting better. So as the mercury level is actually increasing, what we're measuring, she is actually getting better, which means that this person was not able to get rid of the mercury on her own. In fact, this person, even with the appropriate treatments, was not able to get rid of the mercury. This is what we see with autism, and I will explain that just shortly.

You see the continuation of this. On slide No. 19, we've gone from 2.8 to 9.4 to 19 to 27 micrograms per gram creatinin of mercury. This woman at this point was completely normal. She was symptom free.

If you go to slide No. 22, we see what is actually going on here. Michael Godfrey, who is going to be a coauthor with me on the study that we are getting ready to publish, essentially found that there is a genetic predisposition—I believe there is probably a number of them, but the one that he found was apo-E allele, and we confirmed this with our study—but, basically, a genetic predisposition that allows for a person not to be able to detoxify the system as a vast majority of people.

The question is always abundantly made obvious to—it's a recurrent question that's asked all the time in similar hearings and lectures, where people will say that—why is it that one child has this problem and their twin does not have the problem? If it affects one child, it should affect all the children. The point is that they are genetically predisposed. They are a canary. They're sensitive. Their system cannot eliminate the toxicity that they have been exposed to.

Now, on slide 24 is a picture of my son who, fortunately, is here with me; and he will be happy to answer any of the questions after we're done. But at the age of 14 months he lost his speech, he lost his ability to speak, and he had—his first word was "abu" which means father in Arabic and had about another 10-word vocabulary. By the 15th month he had lost his vocabulary after about a week of—about 10 days after his inoculations.

I started his treatments at the age of 3 after we got definitive diagnosis, and you're looking at slide No. 25: No mercury. Slide No. 46: No mercury. Slide No. 27: No mercury.

But Boyd Haley, who I'm sure you're familiar with, Boyd Haley had a very interesting study that came up where they compared normally developing children with children that had autism. And what they found was that children that had autism had no mercury in their hair, whereas children that were developing normally had very high levels of mercury. Why? Because these children can get rid of mercury. That's the whole point. The children that are autistic cannot get rid of it.

You'll see after six tests, on slide 29, is my son's mercury level. You saw four previous slides that showed no mercury, and now you see his mercury level on slide 29 was 13 micrograms per gram creatinin, which is over four times the toxic level.

Today, you will see for yourself what he is capable of doing. He's far ahead of his peers. He is speaking in two different languages. He reads, he writes, he plays chess, and there is nothing that this kid can't do.

We decided to see if this was something just isolated. We did 31 patients we put on the study, all with diagnoses of autism, autism-like spectrum, pervasive developmental delay. They were all treated with the same format, transdermal DMPS with—it's conjugated with a number of different amino acids, and it's delivered in a highly specialized micro-encapsulated liposomal phospolipid transdermal base. All 31 patients were tested at baseline with urine metal screens, hair metal screens, blood metal screens, as well as fecal metal screens; and all children showed little or no mercury on initial testing.

You will see in slide 37 an example of a child that was tested and had nothing that showed up at baseline, but as treatments continued these children started dumping mercury. You'll see on slide 39 a 400 percent increase. This is an average. I picked an average slide. We're right now doing the statistical analysis on this issue, on this study.

And what I am talking about, recovery, I'm talking about full recovery: speech, cognition, ability to interact with others. I have 19 children documented on video that are full—I don't even like to call it remission, because they're not really remissing from anything. We're just cleaning up their system. But they're in normal school.

You would not be able to tell. We have another 30-some children that we have treated that are well on the way of getting better.

The issue here is that—what is the difference between Alzheimer's and autism? There is no difference except of when the exposure was made. In other words, if you take an Alzheimer's patient and have them fast forward into the future, where they were just born 5 years ago, today they would have autism. If you took an autistic children and they were born 70 years ago, today they would have Alzheimer's. The only difference is chronic insidious exposure versus acute load of mercury.

What I am here, hopefully, and on behalf of the parents of the children that I am treating, as well as a number of other physicians that have started using this treatment modality, is to show that the transdermal DMPS is a method of removing mercury, regardless of where it is coming from, and we can get rid of it; and then other new treatments such as nutrition, hyperbarics become even more efficacious in helping to regenerate the neurons that have been damaged from the mercury.

Mr. BURTON. This is very impressive, Doctor. It's hard for a layman like myself—maybe Dr. Watson can do it better—to keep with you when you're going through this. I think I have the gist of it.

What we would like to do, I'd like to submit all this to HHS and CDC to have them take a look at it, let them know that the Congress is watching it. But I'd like to have it—in addition to this, maybe something written out so that the—not only can I follow it thoroughly but so that the people over there at HHS and CDC will not be able to say they couldn't follow it. You see what I am saying.

Dr. BUTTAR. We have given you a 12-page written narrative to go with this, sir. I was also told I had 5 minutes to give a 2-hour presentation.

Mr. BURTON. Well, you did pretty well. You didn't get it in 5, but you did pretty well. You move awful fast. If you could move your feet that fast, you would be an Olympic runner. But it's very well done, very well done. We will use this, and we will submit it to HHS along with your analysis.

[The prepared statement of Dr. Buttar follows:]

Autism, The Misdiagnosis of Our Future Generations
US Congressional Sub-Committee Hearing
May 6, 2004

Rashid A. Buttar, DO, FAAPM, FACAM, FAAIM
Vice Chairman, American Board of Clinical Metal Toxicology
Visiting Scientist, North Carolina State University

Over the last 15 years, the incidence of Autism has rapidly increased in the industrialized nations with the United States and the United Kingdom having the sharpest rise. A lot of the attention has been given regarding the link between mercury and autism, with mercury being the possible factor underlying the etiology of this condition. The issue of whether mercury plays a role in Autism or other neurodevelopmental disorders has been the subject of long debate and extreme political discourse but the evidence is overwhelmingly obvious to even the simplest of intellects once the data is objectively reviewed.

The prevalence of mercury in our society is endemic in nature. The association of mercury with chronic disease in the US "medical literature" exists but is very anemic. However, when searching under Toxline under the ATSDR (Agency of Toxic Substances and Disease Registry), a division of CDC, one finds all scientific literature which also includes didactic literature, NOT just the "medical literature". Not surprisingly to advanced researchers and physicians, the association of mercury to chronic diseases is well documented in the didactic scientific literature.

The search for the association between mercury and cardiovascular disease, the number one killer in the industrialized world, revealed 358 scientific papers exemplifying the relationship. The search for the association between mercury and cancer, the number two killer in the industrialized world, revealed 643 scientific papers exemplifying the relationship. Both of these conditions represent 80% cause of all deaths in the industrialized world, according to the WHO (World Health Organization) as published in 1998. But the association of mercury with neurodegenerative diseases is the most significant, with the references numbering 1445.

The inevitable question is how do we get exposed to mercury? The sources surround us, from mercury amalgams in our teeth, to the contamination of our water sources, inhalation of combustion from fossil fuel, fish that we consume, virtually all vaccinations, and via breast milk, just to name a few. So if mercury is so devastating, why is it allowed to be in our flu shots, vaccines, foods, etc.? This is the "million dollar" question, although it should be evident to the well informed the answer will be somewhere along the money trail.

Increased exposure to mercury through thimerosal containing vaccines is one of the most important issues at hand. Thimerosal (also known as Marthiolate) is the common name of a substance known as ethyl mercurithiosalicylic acid. The overburdening knowledge that thimerosal is converted to ethyl mercury (a substance over a thousand times more destructive than inorganic mercury) in less than one minute after being introduced into the body should give great concern to those appointed to protect the public. Yet, it is virtually ignored. Why is this highly toxic substance still allowed to be a constituent of our vaccines used to inoculate our precious children, our own future generations?

For example, the MSDS on thimerosal from Eli Lilly, documented on their own letter head as far back as July 13, 1991 clearly states that thimerosal is a "product containing a chemical known to the State of California to cause birth defects or other reproductive harm". Yet Eli Lilly continues to use thimerosal in the manufacturing process for vaccines. However, the vaccine issue must not overshadow the cumulative mercury exposure experienced by the patient during gestation and early infancy. These additional exposures besides the vaccine history include dietary mercury content, dental amalgam fillings which contribute greatly to the maternal mercury load, Rhogam (immunoglobulin) administration to mother during gestation, exposure to combustion of fossil fuels, water contamination, and mercuric compounds used in skin products.

Mercury's causes damage by various mechanisms which include: competitive and noncompetitive inhibition of enzyme activity by reversibly or irreversibly binding to active sulfur, binding at the sites off and displacing other divalent cations, like magnesium, zinc, copper, and manganese causing a disruption of enzyme systems, disrupting critical electron transfer reactions, and complexing molecules and inducing a change in structure or conformation which causes them to be perceived as foreign by the body's immune defense and repair system (hapten reactions) resulting in hypersensitivity that can potentiate or exacerbate autoimmune reactions. Mercury alters biological systems because of its affinity for sulfhydryl groups which are functional parts of most enzymes and hormones. Tissues with the highest concentrations of sulfhydryl groups include the brain, nerve tissue, spinal ganglia, anterior pituitary, adrenal medulla, liver, kidney, spleen, lungs heart and intestinal lymph glands.

But most relevant to us for the purposes of this hearing is that mercury has clearly been shown to causes a denudation of the neurofibrils resulting in direct damage to the neuronal cells. In addition, mercury exposure leads to many secondary clinical problems resulting from the aforementioned mechanisms of damage, such as immuno-suppression, allowing for opportunistic infections, allergies, GI dysbiosis, etc. Addressing all other issues in children with Autism is analogous to attempting to put out fires without addressing the cause of the fire itself. The fire will keep re-igniting unless the "spark" is eliminated. It is the elimination of this "spark", i.e. mercury, for which we now have an easy and effective solution. Along with some supportive therapies, Autism and certain other chronic neurodegenerative diseases such as Alzheimer's can be fully and permanently reversed if appropriately treated. This is NOT theory. It has already been clinically validated on a repetitive basis.

But first, let us answer the question why some people are affected while others show no manifestations of mercury toxicity, despite living in the same environments. In our case, the discussion will be limited to mercury, which is considered to be the second most toxic metal known to man but this explanation is applicable to most other heavy metals as well. Most individuals exposed to mercury as well as other heavy metals, have the ability to at least begin the process of eliminating these heavy metal out of their system. But not everyone has this ability and the extent of variability in the ability of an individual to detoxify their systems will determine the severity of the symptoms of toxicity. Slides #10 to #14 show the typical individual who can get rid of mercury with appropriate treatments. Despite having been exposed to severe levels of mercury vapor, this patient named Robin T. was able to detoxify once appropriately treated with DMPS. Her mercury level was almost 22 fold greater or 2200% more than what is considered to be safe but with appropriate treatments, her levels returned to normal and her symptoms of mercury toxicity resolved.

However, patients with impaired detoxification pathways do not show similar results on testing. Their bodies are unable to release the mercury and/or other metals and on testing, the mercury does not appear. The basis of our treatment protocol for children diagnosed with autism was determined by my clinical observation that certain individuals were unable to detoxify mercury like the vast majority of people appear to have the ability to do so. Slides #16 to # 21 show the case of Karen R. who showed no appreciable levels of mercury despite appropriately being "challenged" with DMPS by two different physicians over a year apart. But in Karen R.'s case, she could not detoxify her system effectively despite being treated appropriately with the correct diagnostic methods.

In Karen R's case, she needed to have persistent treatment for a period of almost 2 years, as seen on slides #16 to #21 but as you will notice, her mercury levels continued to exponentially RISE until her last test which shows the results dramatically drop. What is most interesting is that as the test results revealed an increase in the mercury levels, the patient dramatically began to improve clinically. The reason the levels of mercury actually rose in each subsequent test, is that this testing method only determines how MUCH mercury and/or other metals we are able to remove. As treatment continued, we were effectively able to remove a greater quantity of mercury during each and every treatment.

It is important to note that this patient received treatments every week but the test results were obtained only every 20 weeks. Despite this disparity between treatments and testing, we see a dramatic and steady increase in mercury levels on testing, directly correlated with significant improvements clinically and alleviations of symptoms. In this particular patient, the symptoms for which she presented included glactorhea, ataxia, dysphagia, inability to articulate with a new onset of stuttering, arrhythmia, chest pain, myalgias, artharalgias, hirtuism, cephalgia, insomnia, fatigue, malaise, depression, and anxiety. On presentation, the patient had notified me she had seen 16 other physicians in the previous 5 years and if I could NOT help her, she would "take care" of the problems herself because she could no longer live this way. This patient, Karen D. was 34 years old when she presented to me. The level of mercury measured during each of Karen D.'s tests was inversely proportionate to the amount of mercury remaining in her system.

The answer to the question of why some people are able to effectively release mercury and/or show absolutely no manifestations of mercury toxicity despite having lived in the same exact environments and had the same level of exposure to metals while others are severely affected with serious clinical manifestations, is not as difficult to answer as one would initially believe when the multiple variables are considered, which include the type of exposure, biological individuality and genetic predisposition. Drs. Michael Godfrey, et al, reported one such variable explaining the variability of individuals in detoxifying mercury in a landmark paper published in the Journal of Alzheimer's Disease in 2003, entitle "Apolipoprotein E Genotyping as a Potential Biomarker for Mercury Neurotoxicity".

> Apolipoprotein-E (apo-E) genotyping has been investigated as an indicator of susceptibility to heavy metal (i.e., lead) neurotoxicity. Moreover, the apo-E epsilon 4 allele is a major risk factor for neurodegenerative conditions, including Alzheimer's disease (AD). A theoretical biochemical basis for this risk factor is discussed herein, supported by data from 400 patients with presumptive mercury-related neuro-psychiatric symptoms and in whom apo-E determinations were made. A statistically relevant shift toward the at-risk apo-E ϵ 4 groups was found in the patients (...0 001). The patients possessed a mean of 13.7 dental amalgam fillings and 31.5 amalgam surfaces. This far exceeds the number capable of producing the maximum identified tolerable daily intake of mercury from amalgam. The clinical diagnosis and proof of chronic low-level mercury toxicity has been difficult due to the non-specific nature of the symptoms and signs. Dental amalgam is the greatest source of mercury in the general population and brain, blood and urine mercury levels increase correspondingly with the number of amalgams and amalgam surfaces in the mouth. Confirmation of an elevated body burden of mercury can be made by measuring urinary mercury, after provocation with 2,3, dimercapto-propane sulfonate (DMPS) and this was measured in 150 patients. Apo-E genotyping warrants investigation as a clinically useful biomarker for those at increased risk of neuropathology, including AD, when subjected to long-term mercury exposures. Additionally, when clinical findings suggest adverse effects of chronic mercury exposure, a DMPS urine mercury challenge appears to be a simple, inexpensive procedure that provides objective confirmatory evidence. An opportunity could now exist for primary health practitioners to help identify those at greater risk and possibly forestall subsequent neurological deterioration.

We started treating children with Autism first in 1996. By 1997, we were being referred patients by a pediatric neurologist, who was follwing a mutual patient and observed significant changes in the child's behavior after implementation of our treatments. However, by the end of 1998, taking care of children with special needs proved more than I wanted to handle. Although we had far better success than the traditional approach, our treatments had not been responsible for "normalizing" any children. The emotional component was also overwhelming, just having to deal with the pain and frustration of the parents of these children. As a result, we stopped accepting new patients with the diagnosis of Autism or any type of developmental delay in early 1999.

On January 25, 1999, my son Abid Azam Ali Buttar was born. By the time he was 15 months old, he was saying "Abu" which means father in Arabic, and a few other words such as "bye bye". But by the age of 18 months, my son had not only failed to progress in his ability to speak, but had also lost the few words he had been saying. At the age of 36 months, he had absolutely no verbal communication except for the one syllable that he would utter, "deh", on a repetitive basis. As he grew older, I began to worry more and more that he was suffering from a developmental delay. He exhibited the same characteristics that so many parents with children that have developmental delays have observed, such as stemming, walking on tip toes, and lack of eye contact. Sometimes I would call to him but his lack of response would convince me there must be something wrong with his hearing. Certain sounds would make him cringe and he would put his hands on his ears to block the obvious discomfort he was experiencing. He would spend hours watching the oscillation of a fan. But through all this, when he would make eye contact with me, his eyes would say, "I know you can do it Dad". The expression he would give me, for just an instant, would be that of a father encouraging his son.

The oceans of tears that I cried and the hours that I spent trying to figure out what was happening to my son are no different than that of any other parent in the same situation. The only difference was that I was one of only a 190 doctors through out the US board certified in clinical metal toxicology. And if this was metal related, I should know how to fix this problem. I tested him and re-tested him and tested him again, searching for mercury. Slides # 23 to 27 show the results of my son's test and how his system showed no appreciable levels of mercury. But the older he became, the more obvious it became that my son was not developing as he was meant to be developing. My son was not meant to be this way and that was the only one thing that I knew for certain.

About the same time while desperately searching for the cause of the same ailment that had afflicted so many of my own patients previously, I had been invited to present a lecture regarding some of our research on IGF-1 and the correlation with cancer. I had notified the conference that I was too busy to present this lecture but when I learned that Dr. Boyd Haley was also scheduled to present at this conference, I changed my schedule and agreed to lecture just so I could meet and discuss my son's situation with Dr. Haley. That meeting turned out to be one of the key elements which resulted in our development and subsequent current protocol for treating children with autism, autism like spectrum and pervasive developmental delay. My son was the first one who went through this protocol once safety had been established. Dr. Haley told me of a study that had at the time, not yet been published.

Just before the turn of the century, Holmes, Blaxill and Haley did a study assessing the level of mercury measured in the hair of 45 normally developing children versus 94 children with neurodevelopmental delays diagnosed as Autism using DSM IV criteria. The finding showed that the Autistic children had 0.47 parts per million of mercury in their hair where as the normally developing children had 3.63 parts per million, more that 7 times the same level of mercury as the Autistic children. Opponents of the mercury-neurodegeneration camp used this opportunity to state that this study clearly showed that mercury had NOTHING to do with Autism or any other neurodegenerative condition. However, they completely missed the point of the study. For the reader, the conclusion of the study is obvious, and in part, is reproduced below.

> "The reduced levels of mercury in the first baby haircut of autistic infants raise clear questions about the detoxification capacity of a subset of infants. Despite hair levels suggesting low exposure, these infants had measured exposures at least equal to control population, suggesting that control infants were able eliminate mercury more effectively. In the case of autistic infants, those in our sample were exposed to higher levels of mercury during gestation, through dental amalgams or Rho D immunoglobulin injections in the mother. The addition of multiple postnatal exposures to mercury in childhood vaccines would have more severe consequences in infants whose detoxification capacity is reduced or who may be closer to a dangerous threshold exposure. In the case of control infants, mercury hair levels were strongly affected by exposure levels, suggesting that detoxification and excretion played an important role in ensuring normal development in children with elevate toxic exposure relative to peers. If reduced overall mercury elimination is related to hair elimination, then autistic infants will retain significantly higher

> levels of mercury in tissue, including the brain, than normal infants. In light of the biological plausibility of mercury's role in neurodevelopmental disorders, our study provides further insight into one possible mechanism by which early mercury exposures could increase the risk of autism."

These findings were published in the International Journal of Toxicology in 2003. Understanding these findings, along with my clinical experience with the case of Karen D. as previously detailed, led me to the conclusion that a more aggressive method of treatment was necessary compared to the DMSA and various other treatments I had to date employed in the attempt to document high levels of mercury in my son, which up to this point, had not been successful. The first two attempts with DMPS as a challenge treatment were unsuccessful, the first due to difficulty catching the urine since Abie was only 2 years old at the time, and the other due to loss of the urine specimen while being delivered to the laboratory. The third try with DMPS, which represented the 6th test we did on my son with all previous tests showing no appreciable levels of mercury, resulted in the findings on slide #29, the results that were reported to me on his 3rd birthday. His mercury level was over 400% that of safe levels. It is important to note that this level was only indicative of what we were able to "elicit or sequester" out of him. His actual levels were far greater.

I started his treatments on his 3rd birthday, using a rudimentary version of the current TD-DMPS (DMPS in a transdermal base) that my partner, Dr. Dean Viktora and I had played around with a few years previously. By the age of 41 months, 5 months after initiating treatment with the TD-DMPS, my son started to speak, with such rapid progression of his speech that his speech therapist was noted to comment how she had never seen such rapid progress in speech in a child before. Today at the age of 5, Abie is far ahead of his peers, learning prayers in a second language, doing large mathematical calculations in his head, playing chess and already reading simple 3 and 4 letter words. His attention span and focus was sufficiently advanced to the point of being accepted as the youngest child into martial arts academy when he was only 4. His vocabulary is as extensive as any 10 year old's, and his sense of humor, power to reason and ability to understand detailed and complex concepts constantly amazes me. This was the preliminary basis for our study that we initiated, which came about as a result of the extraordinary results obtained in the treatment of my son, Abie.

The Autism study consisted of 31 patients with the diagnoses of autism, autism like spectrum, and pervasive developmental delay. Inclusion criteria was simple, including an independent diagnosis of the above mentioned conditions from either a neurologist or pediatrician, and the desire of the parent to try the treatment protocol using TD-DMPS. All patients were enrolled sequentially as they presented to the clinic and only those who did not wish to participate in the TD-DMPS were not included.

All 31 patients were tested for metal toxicity using four different tests: urine metal toxicity and essential minerals, hair metal toxicity and essential minerals, RBC metal toxicity, and fecal metal toxicity, all obtained from Doctor's Data Laboratory. These tests were performed at baseline, and repeated at 2 months, 4 months, 6 months, 8 months, 10 months, 12 months, and then every 4 months there after. All 31 patients showed little or no level of mercury on the initial baseline test results. Slide #37 shows an example of a baseline test result of one participant in the study showing very little mercury. In addition, all study patients had chemistries, CBC with differentials, lipid panels, iron, thyroid profiles and TSH drawn every 60 days. Further specialized testing also included organic acid testing (OAT test) from Great Plains Laboratory and complete diagnostic stool analysis (CDSA) from Doctor's Data Laboratory. If indicated, IgG mediated food allergy testing was also obtained but was not routinely performed.

Compared to the baseline results all 31 patients showed significantly higher levels of mercury as treatment continued. Slide #39 shows significantly higher mercury levels in this same study patient after two months of treatment with the TD-DMPS, with results showing approximately a 350% increase from previous baseline levels. The improvements in the patients in the study correlated with increased yield in measured mercury levels upon subsequent testing. Essentially, what was noted was that as more mercury was eliminated, the more noticeable the clinical improvements and the more dramatic the change in the patient.

The manifestations of this evidence for clinical improvements included many observations but were specifically quantifiable with some patients who had no prior history of speech starting to speak at the age of 6 or 7, sometimes in full sentences. Patients also exhibited substantially improved behavior, reduction and eventual cessation of all stemming behavior, return of full eye contact, and rapid potty training, sometimes in children that were 5 or 6 but had never been successfully potty trained. Additional findings reported by parents included improvement and increase in rate of physical growth increased, as well as the child beginning to follow instructions, becoming affectionate and social with siblings or other children, seeking interaction with others, appropriate in response, and a rapid acceleration of verbal skills. The results in many of these children has been documented on video and other physicians involved with this protocol have been successfully able to reproduce the same results.

DMPS, or dimercaptopropane – 1 sulfonate, is a primary chelator for mercury and arsenic. Slide 42 shows the chemical structure of DMPS. DMPS has pitfalls as well as advantages. The pitfalls include oral dosing which is the usual recommended dosing because it is approximately 50% to 55% absorbed by the gastrointestinal mucosa. As a result of already compromised gastrointestinal function and dysbiosis noted in most of these children, there is also be a decreased absorption of the DMPS when dosed orally, and with the severe gut vacillations prevalent in our society, DMPS by mouth becomes impractical. Most of the children that have taken the DMPS orally for more than 1 week continuously, begin complaining of abdominal pain, cramping and other GI distress. We tried the oral DMPS for almost 6 weeks before eliminating it as a possible therapeutic method. Intravenous methods of application were not an option in children so young, although is the preferred method I have used in my clinical practice for my adult patients with mercury toxicity.

All study patients were also monitored for renal function, and mineral depletion. The key to success with this study was the constant and continuous "pull" of mercury by being able to dose it every other day and the compliance of patient and parents. Each patient was put on a protocol consisting of the transdermal DMPS (TD-DMPS). Transdermal DMPS is

DMPS conjugated with a number of amino acids, delivered in highly specialized micro-encapsulated liposomal phospholipid transdermal base with essential fatty acids. The frequent dosing is one of the most important components of the TD-DMPS. It is important to note that DMPS is highly oxygen reactive and is very unstable when exposed to air. This and many other issues of delivery, stabilization, and oxidation have all been successfully identified and resolved over the last two years with the final result now pending patent. In addition, certain other components have been added to the TD-DMPS to potentiate the efficacy of treatment, such as the addition of various amino acids and glutathione.

There are a number of agents that have been demonstrated to have clinical utility in facilitating the removal of mercury from someone who has demonstrated clinical signs and symptoms of mercury toxicity. The most important part of this systemic elimination process, however, is the removal of the source of mercury. Once this has been completed, treatment for systemic mercury detoxification can begin. The following is a summary of the most effective agent as well as the most commonly used agent that have been documented in the peer-reviewed literature.

A. <u>DMPS</u>

1. The chemical name is Sodium 2,3 dimercaptopropane-1-sulfonate, this water soluble dimercaprol has 2 active sulfhydryl sites that form complexes with heavy metals such as zinc, copper, arsenic, mercury, cadmium, lead sliver, and tin.

2. The chemical structure of DMPS is:

```
CH2 – CH – CH2 – S – O3 – NA
 |     |
 SH    SH
```

3. DMPS was developed in the 1950's by the Soviets as an antidote for the chemical warfare agent Lewisite.

    3. It became commercially available in 1978, being produced by the German pharmaceutical company Heyl.

    4. There has been extensive research in both safety and effectiveness of this drug in the 50 years of its existence and it is now considered to be the most effective therapy for the treatment of mercury toxicity, as mercury is bound to sulfur groups throughout the body and is therefore difficult to remove. The sulfur groups on this compound readily unseat the mercury from its attachment to sulfur in our tissues, then this compound is excreted through the kidneys unchanged.

    5. DMPS is widely available throughout the United States as a compounded bulk drug and has been recognized by the FDA in that capacity.

6. DMPS is very safe when used properly. Side effects are very rare, but may include allergic reactions such as skin rashes. Most important is to monitor and supplement with appropriate doses of zinc and copper as these minerals are bound readily by DMPS in the same way as it binds mercury. This should be done prior to commencement of any DMPS treatment regimen, then periodically throughout the process.

7. DMPS can be taken orally, as over 50% is absorbed. Most trained chelation physicians in the United States utilize intravenous challenges, whereas most European physicians will challenge with oral DMPS.

8. Currently, the only professional medical organizations that teach and certify physicians in chelation therapy are the International College of Integrative Medicine and the American College for Advancement of Medicine. Both of these organizations periodically conduct workshops on mercury toxicity specifically with emphasis on both basic science knowledge and clinical evaluation and treatment.

9. With the increased concern of mercury toxicity as an environmental health threat and in recognition of the need to increase basic science research and clinical treatment of heavy metal toxicity, the American Board of Clinical Metal Toxicology was recently formed as an evolution of the American Board of Chelation Therapy. This Board will now expand greatly the educational opportunities for physicians interested in this health problem and offer certification procedures that will expand even further the work that has already been done.

10. As a result of the work of these organizations, a general protocol for the use of DMPS has been established which most certified physicians follow.

B. <u>DMSA</u>

1. 2,3 dimercaptosuccinic acid is also a dithiol, like DMPS, and therefore is more effective that EDTA in removing mercury.
2. Structure:

```
HOOC – C  –  C – COOH
       |     |
       SH    SH
```

3. This chelator is an oral agent that is reportedly effective in removing both lead and mercury and is used frequently to treat children.
4. DMSA removes mercury both by way of the kidneys, though urine, and the liver, through bile and then the intestines. .
5. DMSA has several disadvantages but also some advantages relative to DMPS:

   a. DMPS remains in the body for a longer time than DMSA, therefore it is able to more thoroughly bind to mercury and eliminate greater amounts per treatment.
   b. DMPS acts more quickly than DMSA.
   c. DMPS is given intravenously, intramuscularly, or orally while DMSA is strictly an oral preparation.
6. DMSA is now thought to be potentially harmful if used in patients with excessively high levels of mercury. Therefore, DMSA is recommended for use only late in the mercury elimination process after the peripheral tissue load of mercury has been reduced by DMPS.

In our observation, DMSA did not show efficacy in removing mercury. Slides #26 and #29 show a comparison in the effect of pulling out mercury, completed less than 30 days apart in my son's case. The yield of DMPS compared to DMSA for removal of mercury in this example was 10 to 1. There is an intriguing explanation provided by Boyd Haley, DSc, to support my clinical observations to the lack of efficacy observed with the use of DMSA in treating children with autism and developmental delays. DMSA stands for dimercapto-succinic acid. Succinic acid is a major substrate in the citric acid cycle and DMSA is an analog of succinic acid.

Therefore, DMSA would most likely act as an inhibitor of the enzyme in the citric acid cycle that uses succinic acid as a substrate. This would result in DMSA actually acting as a competitive inhibitor of succinic acid and in turn, would lead to a slowing down of, or inhibition of the citric acid cycle. Succinate produces FADH2 which is directly coupled to the electron transport chain and leads to ATP production. The competitive inhibition of this succinic acid by DMSA would thus, eventually result in an inhibition of ATP production leading to decreased energy utilization causing a significant burden and impaired ability of the physiological system to function correctly.

In our clinical experience, the only effective method that has resulted in the consistent removal of mercury resulting in the elimination of this "spark" in the pediatric population is the TD-DMPS that was originally formulated only for the purposes of treating my son's developmental delay. Since it's implementation, we have now successfully treated scores of patients, many of whom have completely recovered but all of whom have improved since the implementation of this treatment. These results have been duplicated by other physicians involved with the care of patients with neurodegenerative disease processes.

Children with Autism (mercury toxicity) have many resulting imbalances in their systems, including but not limited to significant allergies, systemic candidiasis, hormonal imbalances, gastrointestinal dysbiosis, immune dysfunctions, nutritional deficiencies, etc. However these are what I refer to as the "fires" of autism. All these, and other "fires" of autism result from one "spark". Mercury! Successfully addressing many or all of these "fires" will accomplish transient improvement but until the "spark" that constantly re-ignites these "fires" has definitively been eliminated, any improvement will be short lived at best. Mercury is NOT the fire. It is however, the spark that ignites and constantly re-ignites these "fires". In addition, this particular patient population seems to have antibodies to mercury binding fibrillarin, confirming the fact that mercury is the cause. But it's the spark, not the fire. Until the spark is eradicated, the fire will continue to re-start and damage the brain and other vital areas such as the immune system. Mercury is the underlying common denominator of all the problems from which these children suffer.

Children diagnosed with autism suffer from acute mercury toxicity secondary to huge exposure while in utero (maternal amalgam load, dietary factors, maternal inoculations, Rhogam injections, etc.) and early on in life (vaccinations preserved with thimerosal, etc.). Adults diagnosed with Alzheimer's suffer from chronic, insidious mercury toxicity secondary to exposure over a long time (amalgam load, inhalation of mercury vapors, combustion of fossil fuels, dietary factors, etc.). By addressing and eliminating the mercury "spark", these secondary "fires" become far easier to manage clinically and the improvements realized from treatment of the resulting imbalances become easier to maintain.

Mercury directly causes damage to the neuronal cell resulting in denudation of the neurofibrils. In addition, mercury results in secondary problems as discussed such as immuno-suppression, allowing for opportunistic infections, allergies, GI dysbiosis, etc. Addressing all other issues such as immuno-suppression in children with Autism without addressing the issue of mercury, is analogous to attempting to put out multiple fires without addressing the arsonist. The fire will keep re-igniting unless the "spark" is eliminated. It is the elimination of this "spark", i.e. mercury, for which we now have an easy and effective solution. Along with some supportive therapies, autism and certain other neurodegenerative diseases can be fully and permanently reversed. This is NOT a theory but rather, a protocol that has already been clinically validated and the evidence is irrefutable.

The reason for some individuals to have severe damage from mercury where others do not have serious adverse neurological deficits extends due to various factors which include biological individuality and genetic predisposition. In addition, what type of toxicity exposure the individual was exposed to, was it inhaled, ingested, or exposed on their skin? What type of mercury exposure did the individual receive? Was it organic or inorganic mercury? If it was organic, was it ethyl mercury or methyl mercury? How frequent was the exposure to the source of toxicity? Was there a significant maternal load present prior to birth? Was the situation exacerbated by the mother being inoculated, or having Rhogam administration. How many administrations took place and over what period of time? What about the diet? How about the proximity to industrial sites, and exposure to combustion of fossil fuel? As you can see, the variables are extensive. But the treatment is essentially the same. The only difference is the extent of continuity of treatment.

Slide 47 shows a newspaper article in the Charlotte Observer with a picture showing one of my patient's mother administering transdermal DMPS to her son's forearms. Slide 48 gives more information on metal toxicity and represents the focus of the majority of my post graduate medical career revolving around the issue of the effective clinical treatment of heavy metal toxicity.

Summary:

The underlying common denominator in chronic neurodegenerative disease seems to be either decreasing vascular supply (less blood to the brain) or accumulation of heavy metals, specifically mercury. The inability of an individual to eliminate toxic metals, especially mercury, is directly related to the level of neurodegeneration experienced. In the young patient population suffering from Autism or Pervasive Developmental Delay, the vascular supply is not an issue. The underlying pathology of children with autism and the geriatric population with Alzheimer's is of the same etiology, specifically mercury toxicity.

Both these patient populations suffer from the inability to excrete mercury as a result of a genetic predisposition resulting from the Apo E allele. This allele appears to be associated with the inability to get rid of mercury from the system. If these patient populations inhabited a complete mercury free environment, they would not have the problems associated with autism or Alzheimer's. When the mercury is successfully removed from their systems, these individuals begin to significantly improve due to a cessation of the destruction and denudation of the neurofibrils, as evidenced by steady improvement in cognitive function.

Mercury is the "spark" that causes the "fires" of Autism as well as Alzheimer's. Autism is the result of high mercury exposure early in life versus Alzheimer's is a chronic accumulation of mercury over a life time. A doctor can treat ALL the "fires" but until the "spark" is removed, there is minimal hope of complete recovery with most improvements being transient at best. However, once the process of mercury removal has been effectively started, the damage is curtailed and full recovery becomes possible and enhanced by utilizing various additional therapies including nutrition, hyperbarics, etc.

Rashid A. Buttar, DO, FAAPM, FACAM, FAAIM
drbuttarclinic@aol.com

Full submission of testimony with supporting data and references to follow.

AUTISM : The MISDIAGNOSIS of Our Future Generations
US Congressional Sub-Committee Hearing
Washington DC
May 6, 2004
Rashid A. Buttar, DO
FAAPM, FACAM, FAAIM
Vice Chairman, American Board of Clinical Metal Toxicology
Visiting Scientist – North Carolina State University
1
Rashid A. Buttar, DO, FAAPM, FACAM, FAAIM

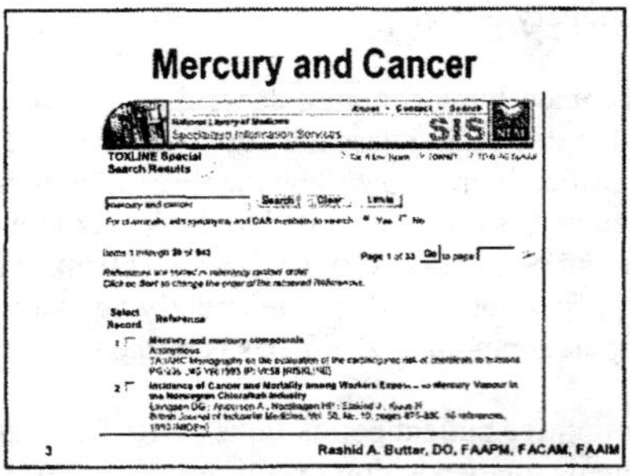
Mercury and Cancer
SIS
TOXLINE Special
Search Results
3
Rashid A. Buttar, DO, FAAPM, FACAM, FAAIM

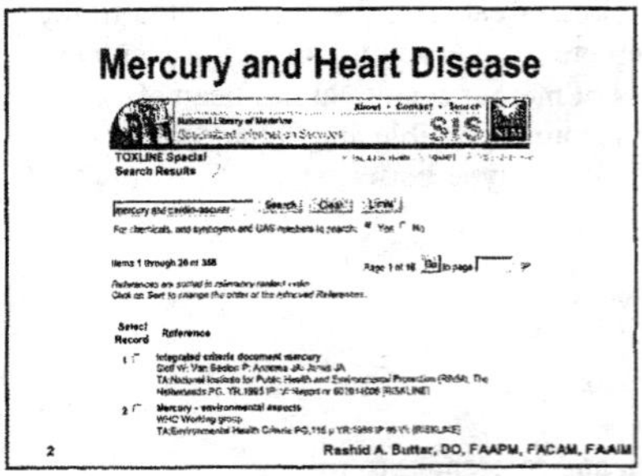
Mercury and Heart Disease
SIS
TOXLINE Special
Search Results
2
Rashid A. Buttar, DO, FAAPM, FACAM, FAAIM

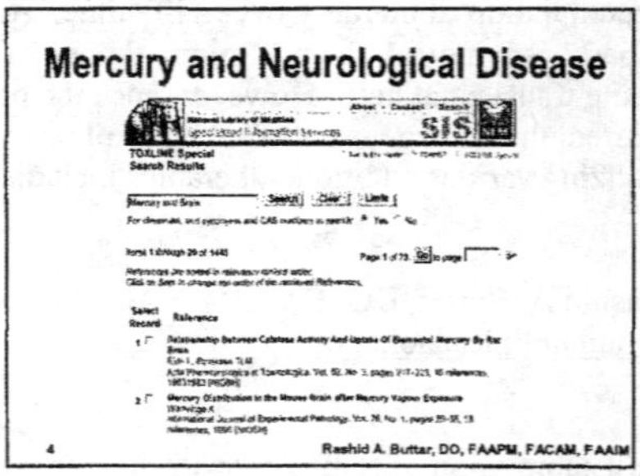
Mercury and Neurological Disease
SIS
TOXLINE Special
Search Results
4
Rashid A. Buttar, DO, FAAPM, FACAM, FAAIM

Pitfalls

Missed Heavy Metals (Especially Mercury)

9 Reshid A. Buttar, DO, FAAPM, FACAM, FAAIM

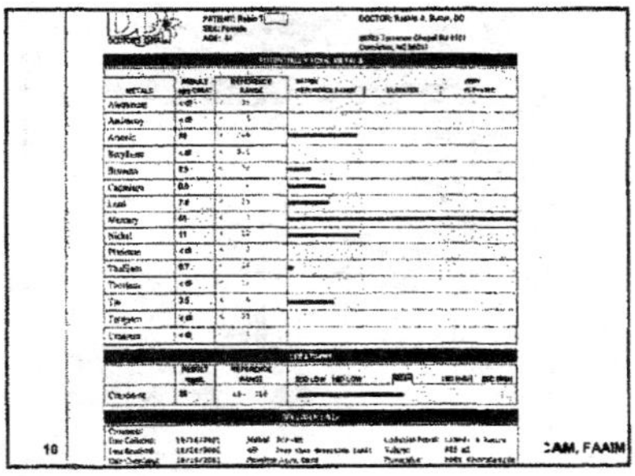
10

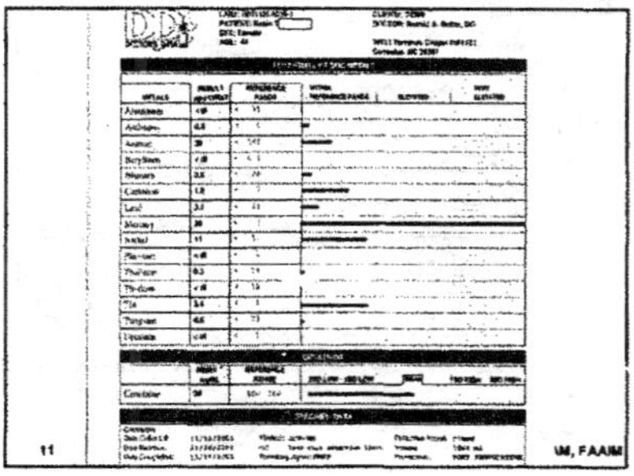
11

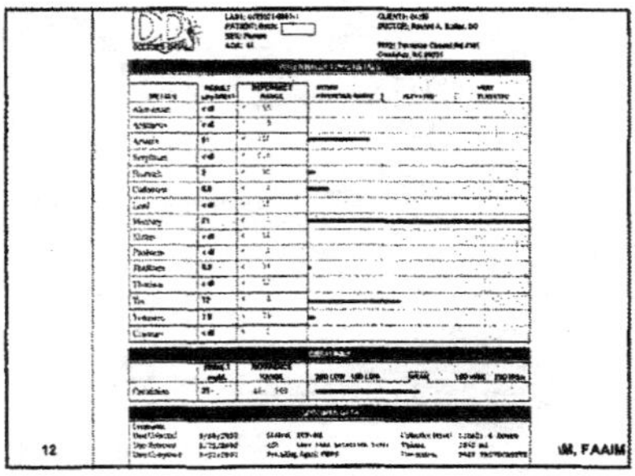
12

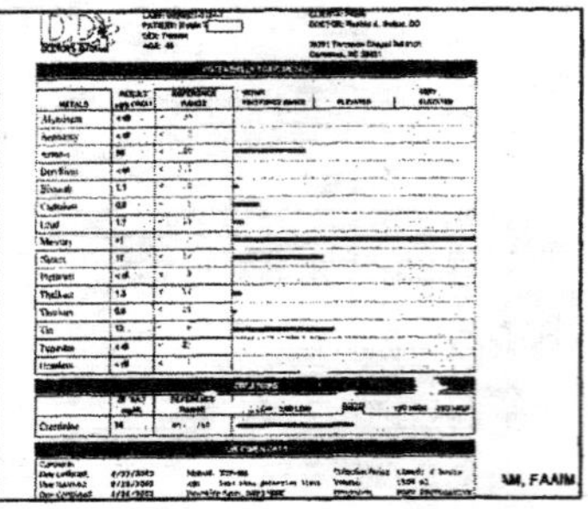

13 ... AM, FAAIM

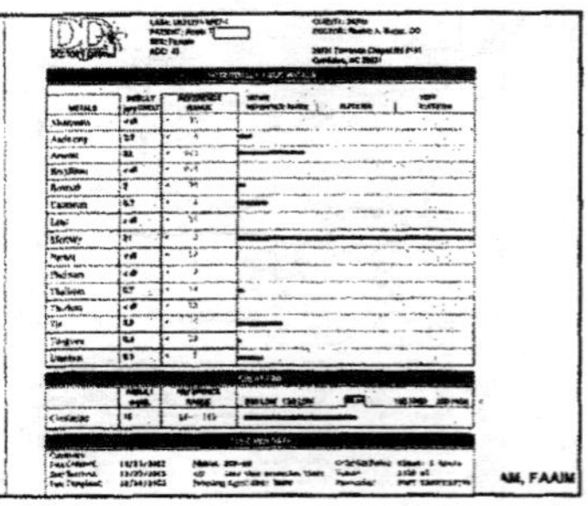

14 ... AM, FAAIM

Pitfalls

Patients with Impaired Detoxification Pathways

15 Rashid A. Buttar, DO, FAAPM, FACAM, FAAIM

16 ... M, FAAIM

Urine Toxic Elements
ELEMENTS REGARDED AS TOXIC
Elements
17
\M, FAAIM

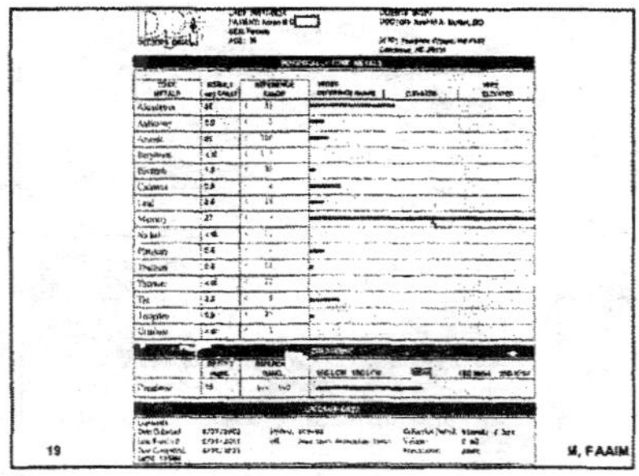
19
M, FAAIM

Urine Toxic Elements
ELEMENTS REGARDED AS TOXIC
Elements
18
\M, FAAIM

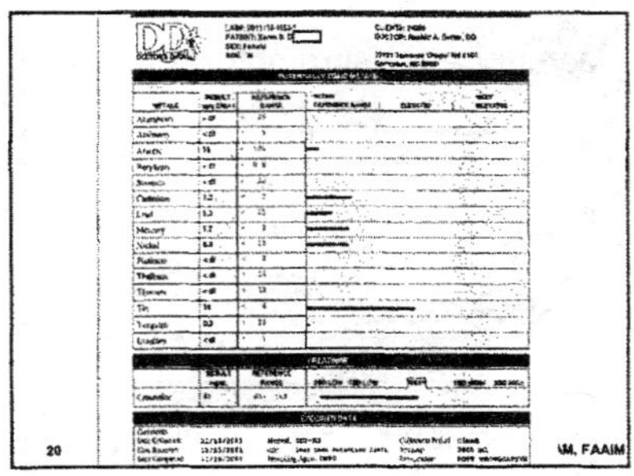
20
\M, FAAIM

Pitfalls

Selected Case Studies Children with "Developmental Delays"

Mercury and Neurological Disease

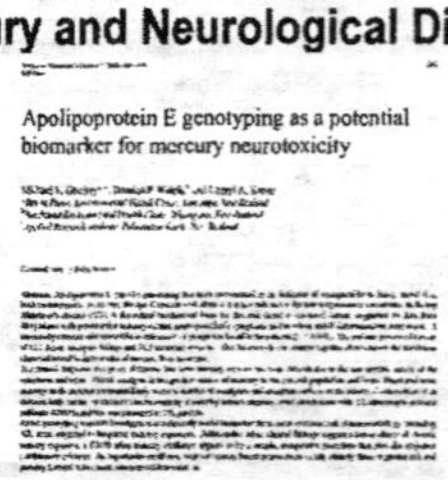

Apolipoprotein E genotyping as a potential biomarker for mercury neurotoxicity

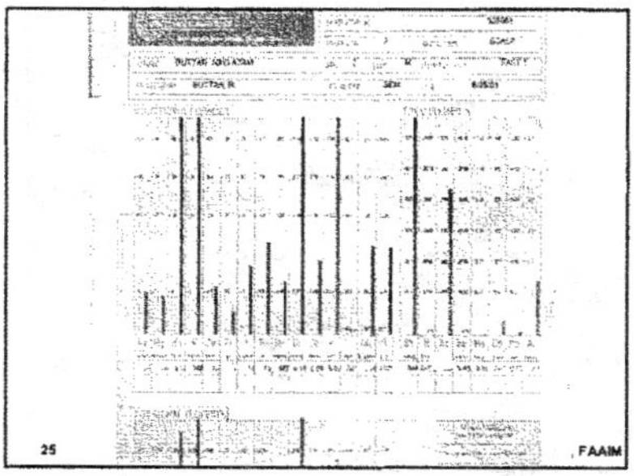
25
FAAIM

HAIR ELEMENTS
27
AAIM

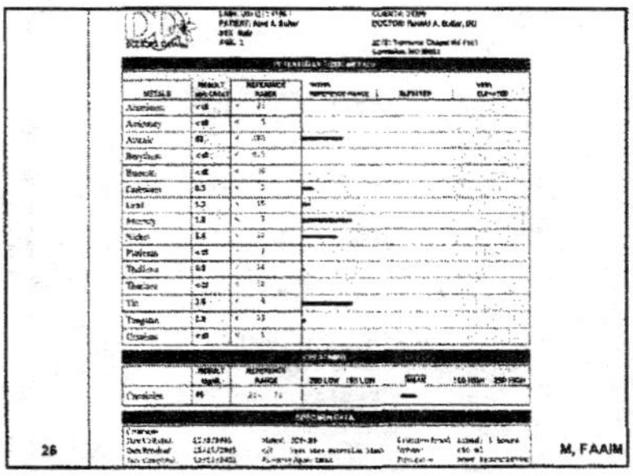
26
M, FAAIM

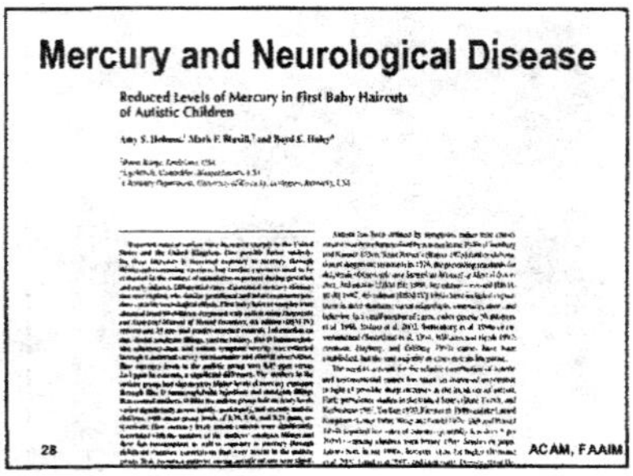
Mercury and Neurological Disease
Reduced Levels of Mercury in First Baby Haircuts of Autistic Children
28
ACAM, FAAIM

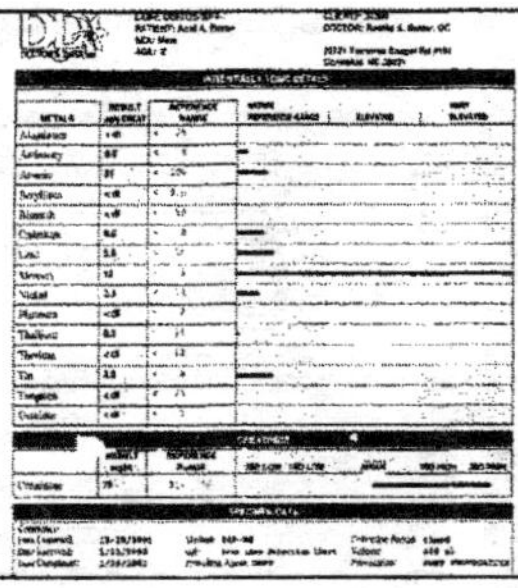

29 M, FAAIM

30 Rashid A. Buttar, DO, FAAPM, FACAM, FAAIM

Posted on Sun, Jun. 29, 2003

The Charlotte Observer

Toddlers could be tested for mercury

States seek grants to address threat posed by toxic metal found in fish

BRUCE HENDERSON
Staff Writer

ON THE WACCAMAW RIVER - After more than a decade of measuring mercury in fish, water and air, Carolinas officials will seek grants this week to test a final frontier: people.

Thousands of people on the coastal plain, where mercury most commonly takes a toxic form, would be tested if the Centers for Disease Control and Prevention approves the grants. Many in Piedmont counties east of Charlotte would be tested, too.

Even without a CDC grant, South Carolina hopes to forge ahead with plans to test 12,000 toddlers, who are at special risk.

In North Carolina, a state toxicologist estimates 7,40u children born each year are already at risk from mercury. In its most toxic form, it can cause neurological damage to developing fetuses and harm the way children think, learn and problem-solve.

31 Rashid A. Buttar, DO, FAAPM, FACAM, FAAIM

Autism Study

31 patients with diagnosis:

Autism

Autism Like Spectrum

Pervasive Developmental Delay

32 Rashid A. Buttar, DO, FAAPM, FACAM, FAAIM

Key To Success - Protocol

Transdermal DMPS (TD-DMPS)
DMPS conjugated with a number of amino acids, delivered in a highly specialized micro-encapsulated liposomal phospholipid transdermal base

33 Rashid A. Buttar, DO, FAAPM, FACAM, FAAIM

Autism Study

All 31 patients tested:

- Urine Metal Toxicity & Essentials
- Hair Metal Toxicity & Essentials
- RBC Metal Toxicity
- Fecal Metal Toxicity

34 Rashid A. Buttar, DO, FAAPM, FACAM, FAAIM

Autism Study

All tests in all 31 patients performed:

Baseline	8 months
2 months	10 months
4 months	12 months,
6 months	then q 4 months

35 Rashid A. Buttar, DO, FAAPM, FACAM, FAAIM

Autism Study

All 31 patients showed LITTLE or NO level of mercury on initial baseline test results

36 Rashid A. Buttar, DO, FAAPM, FACAM, FAAIM

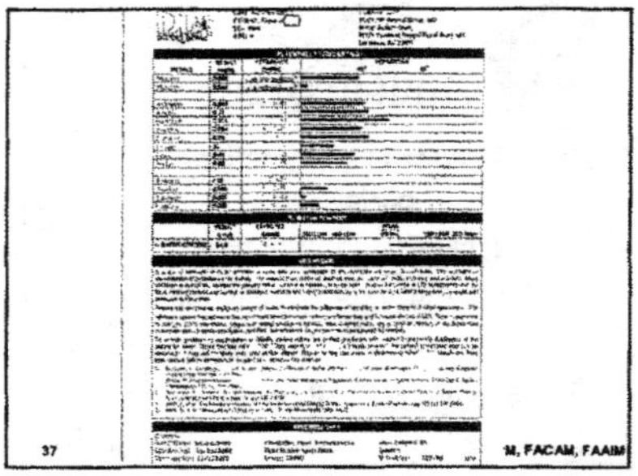

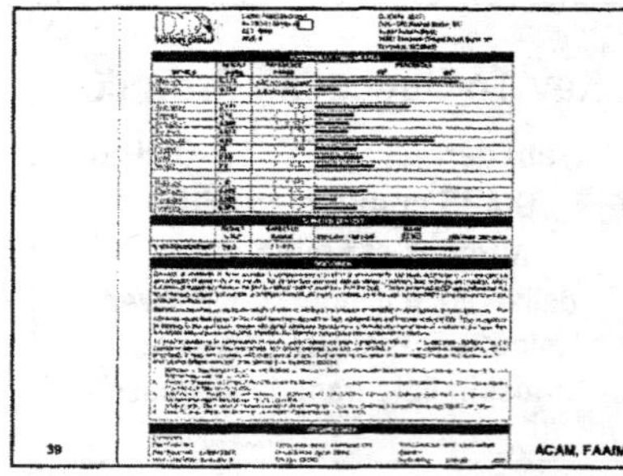

Autism Study

All 31 patients showed significantly higher levels of mercury as treatment continued, compared to baseline test results

38 Rashid A. Buttar, DO, FAAPM, FACAM, FAAIM

Autism Study

Improvements correlate with increase in measured mercury levels, ie, as more mercury was eliminated, the more noticeable the clinical improvements.

40 Rashid A. Buttar, DO, FAAPM, FACAM, FAAIM

Autism Study

Evidence of clinical improvements:

From NO speech to speaking in full sentences / Improved behavior / No stemming / Return of full eye contact / Become potty trained / Physical rate of growth increases / Begin to follow instructions / Appropriate in response

41 Rashid A. Buttar, DO, FAAPM, FACAM, FAAIM

Pitfalls

Oral Dosing
(as usually recommended)

43 Rashid A. Buttar, DO, FAAPM, FACAM, FAAIM

Treatment Protocol

DMPS is primary chelator for mercury

- Sodium 2,3 dimercaptopropane-1-sulfonate
- The chemical structure of DMPS is:

```
CH2 - CH - CH2 - S - O3 - NA
 |     |
SH    SH
```

(Campbell 1986)

Pitfalls

Only 50% GI Absorption
Abnormal GI Function
Severe Gut Vacillation

44 Rashid A. Buttar, DO, FAAPM, FACAM, FAAIM

Pitfalls

Monitor Patient for:

Renal Function

Mineral Depletion

45 Rashid A. Buttar, DO, FAAPM, FACAM, FAAIM

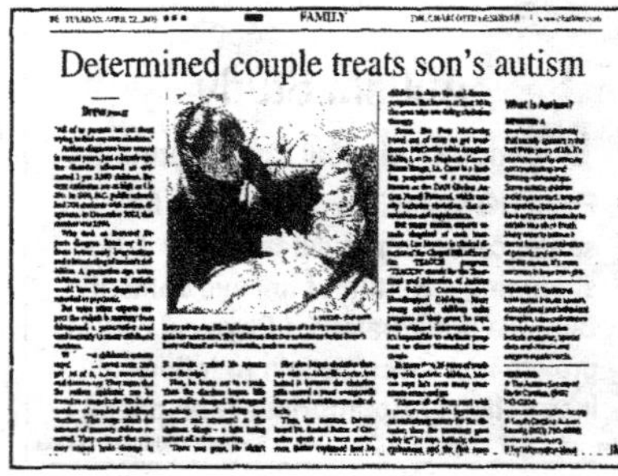
Determined couple treats son's autism

Key To Success

Constant and continuous "pull" of mercury

Issues of Compliance

Frequent Dosing

46 Rashid A. Buttar, DO, FAAPM, FACAM, FAAIM

There is
NO CONTROVERSY

The failure of others to recognize facts does not change the truth.

49 Rashid A. Buttar, DO, FAAPM, FACAM, FAAIM

For those who fight for the truth, remember...

"Each progressive spirit is opposed by a thousand mediocre minds appointed to guard the past." *-Maurice Maeterlinck*

...and that truth will always sustain itself.

50 Rashid A. Buttar, DO, FAAPM, FACAM, FAAIM

Mr. BURTON. Dr. Harch.

Dr. HARCH. Chairman Burton and distinguished members of the committee, thank you for this wonderful opportunity to speak before you today.

Before I get started, I wanted to make an announcement. The International Hyperbaric Medical Association and American Board of Clinical Metal Toxicology as well as Oklahoma University Health Science Center and School of Medicine is going to conduct the first evidence-based medicine study on the only two effective therapies that have been identified for autism: Hyperbaric Oxygen Therapy and chelation therapy. We're going to have an Internet-based study that will allow us to enter patients with autism from all over the country. What we're proposing to do is do a sequence of chelation therapy, hyperbaric oxygen chelation and hyperbaric oxygen, with testing before and after treatment.

As Dr. Bob Nash and I have pointed out, this is the only study that will address two of the major underlying problems with the majority of autism cases: No. 1, the poisoning and stunning of neurons by mercury; and, second, the rebuilding of a stunted brain with hyperbaric oxygen.

I wanted to point out that the State of Wisconsin has recently announced a retraining program for autistic children. It's a 3-year program, $30,000 per child per year. And, unfortunately, at the end of 3 years we're going to spend $90,000 per child; and the children will still be autistic, with maybe some improvement in behavior.

The problem is that the central flaw—you cannot retrain a stunned, stunted brain and poisoned brain. What we're going to do for $20,000 is be able to treat these children with this combination therapy and likely return a substantial number of them to near normal function and better lives.

A word about how I got into this. I made a discovery back in the late 1980's and early 1990's treating our divers in New Orleans with brain decompression illness. Specifically, what we found was divers who had failed standard U.S. Navy treatment and months to years later were disabled by neurocognitive problems, I was able to bring back and subject to a lower pressure protocol of Hyperbaric Oxygen Therapy and improve them dramatically. We used functional brain imaging before and after a hyperbaric treatment to identify that injured area of brain that could respond with a repetitive course of treatment and then document it with a repeat scan.

Well, we then extended that: patients with boxing injury, other causes of traumatic brain injury, chronic stroke, cerebral palsy—the first cerebral palsy cases treated in North America were treated at our facility in 1992 and 1993—toxic brain injury, and then, of course, autism.

In the course of 15 years and approximately 400 patients now we've had about 20 patients with Autism Spectrum Disorders, persistent developmental delay and autism; and what we found is three things.

No. 1, there seem to be in a lot of these children a low blood pressure, low oxygen, low blood flow insult to the brain either in late pregnancy, at the time of birth, or shortly after birth that was either unappreciated, obscured or, frankly, covered up. Second, much of the brain injury we saw was at the base of the brain involving the temporal lobes. And, third, that these children could be improved with hyperbaric oxygen, although we wouldn't cure them.

So over the course of these years we found the autistic children responded much like the divers, the trauma patients, and all the other now 50 different neuropathologies that we have treated; and there's a reason for it. But essentially what I am here to tell you is we have a treatment for brain injury that will revolutionize the treatment of brain injury in the world.

As I told Chairman Regula last week in testimony before his committee, it has now been shown with over 40 years of research that a single high pressure hyperbaric oxygen treatment at the time of a low blood flow, low oxygen insult to the brain can nearly completely negate the effect of that insult. So had my autistic children been treated likely at the time of that injury, they wouldn't be autistic today.

In fact, this is suggested by a study that was done in 1963 and published in the world-famous Lancet by Dr. Hutchinson in England. He took 65 babies born not breathing who failed resuscitation, and when everything failed he put them in a hyperbaric chamber, gave them a single hyperbaric treatment. At the end of the day, 54 percent of them were discharged from the hospital, "apparently well." We know now that this could treat the vast majority of injuries to human beings in the world.

Unfortunately, if you're a child, the only way you can get this is—you can't get it. You have to be a high-priced thoroughbred racehorse newborn foal that is affected by low oxygen and blood flow in Lexington, KY, or Florida and you'll get in a hyperbaric chamber for your injury.

So we also have a treatment for chronic brain injury, and we've shown that, and amongst those are the autistic children.

So, in summary, what I want to tell you is we have a preventative treatment for autism, and we have a treatment for autism. It's hyperbaric oxygen. Combined with chelation therapy such as Dr. Buttar's, we believe we can return the substantial majority of children in the Untied States and the world to improved levels of near normal function; and we are going to prove it in the next 3 years with this evidence-based study.

Thank you so much.

Mr. BURTON. That's very good news as well. And I presume we have detailed analysis and testimony that we can use and also submit to the health agencies.

Dr. HARCH. They've seen it.

Mr. BURTON. Well, they'll see it again.

Dr. HARCH. Good. In fact, Mr. Chairman, I presented this to the MIND Institute in Sacramento a few years ago; and they were not particularly interested. We're hoping they might be more.

Mr. BURTON. We'll send it to the powers that be over there with a personal letter, hopefully from myself and Ms. Watson; and we'll try to make sure that they take a look at it.

Dr. HARCH. Thank you.

[The prepared statement of Dr. Harch follows:]

Testimony

"Announcement of a New Treatment Protocol for Autism Spectrum Disorders and other Neurological Impairments"

The International Hyperbaric Medical Association Foundation

Paul Harch, M.D.

President

INTERNATIONAL HYPERBARIC MEDICAL ASSOCIATION
IHMA
FOUNDATION

Before the

Government Reform & Oversight Hearing --Subcommittee on Wellness & Human Rights

Entitled

"Autism Spectrum Disorders: An Update of Federal Government Initiatives and Revolutionary New Treatments of Neurodevelopmental Diseases "

United States House of Representatives

May 6, 2004, 2:00PM

International Hyperbaric Medical Association Foundation
46 Draper Circle, Suite B   Stafford, Virginia 22554-4754
Office: 540-720-4255   Fax: 540-720-2486

TESTIMONY OF PAUL G. HARCH, M.D
MAY 6, 2004
GOVERNMENT OVERSIGHT COMMITTEE
SUBCOMMITTEE ON HEALTH AFFAIRS
CHAIRMAN, DAN BURTON

Chairman Burton and distinguished members of the Subcommittee, thank you for the opportunity to present the findings of my research and practice on the hyperbaric oxygen therapy (HBOT) treatment of children with autism, autism spectrum disorders, and persistent developmental delay. These findings will hopefully be encouraging, and when coupled with the testimony of the other physicians, exciting. Together we would like to suggest a new approach to the acute treatment of the insults that predispose to these disorders as well as the delayed treatment when the disorder is well established.

The key announcement today is about an evidence-based medicine study that will combine two treatments that have been found to be effective in treating autistic children – mercury detoxification and hyperbaric oxygen. The IHMA Foundation is collaborating with the American Board of Clinical Metal Toxicology (ABCMT) under the supervision of the Oklahoma University Health Sciences Center on this revolutionary new treatment for autism. The Institutional Review Board (IRB) approved protocol will use transdermal DMPS chelation and hyperbaric oxygen. Transdermal DMPS, with absorption through the skin, has a number of advantages over oral, IV, or injected chelation which enhances its effectiveness. After several months on the transdermal chelator, hyperbaric oxygen treatments will be administered using the Neubauer-Harch dive protocol, and then after another time period has elapsed, the second set of HBOT treatments will be administered.

The transdermal chelator will continue to be used until the next set of hyperbaric treatments is applied. It is expected that the combination of the two therapies will double the effectiveness of the chelator and allow the hyperbaric oxygen to cause permanent neural recovery. All patients enrolled in the study will have extensive before and after neurological scans and neuropsych testing performed by independent observers, and all will receive real treatment. After all, no placebo group is necessary when you know the outcome for untreated patients. By definition neither oxygen or the chelator can be a placebo since both have known effects as a drug.

Rashid Buttar, DO, whom you just heard testify, developed this transdermal chelator and has had excellent success with the treatment of over 40 patients. Dr. Buttar is one of the Board members of the IHMA Foundation and also Vice Chairman of the ABCMT.

Dr. Buttar's treatment has clear and demonstrable effects as we can all see here today. The older a child is, however, the more difficulty they have clearing their brain. Bob Nash, MD, Chairman of the ABCMT is a neurologist and certified in chelation and hyperbaric medicine. He explained that you often have to 'pound away' with chelation at patients for a long time because the neurons are stunned and do not have proper metabolism, so they cannot clear the heavy metals and cells cannot pick up the chelate. The addition, hyperbaric treatments kick start the neurons and 'light them up' so when the chelator is present it becomes easier to eliminate the heavy metals that are preventing the neuron's normal function. We expect this combination of therapies to shorten the time that these patients will have to be treated, returning them to more normal status more quickly, and also result in a more complete recovery than if they had each individual treatment by itself.

Dr. Nash came to this conclusion when he examined the brain scans of several of my patients where I used a scan-dive-scan diagnostic to determine recoverable brain tissue. I will cover this evidence in just a moment.

This treatment is available now on a limited basis. Due to collaboration between the IHMA Foundation, Oklahoma University Health Sciences Center, and the treating physicians who have developed this therapy, we expect it to be available in many locations across the nation later this year. After that we expect it to become the standard of care for all autistic children, nation-wide.

Consider that Wisconsin is spending $30,000 in tax dollars on each autistic child per year right now in a special "training program," with a 3 year cost of $90,000 that still leaves children autistic at the end. The outcome is some behavioral improvement. Our treatment program is expected to cost about $20,000 and result in children who can function normally. We expect the states to adopt this protocol quickly and help fund the general treatment for these children once they see the results of this study.

Amongst the nearly 400 brain injured patients that I have evaluated and treated in the past 15 years with HBOT and SPECT are approximately 20 children with Autism, Autism Spectrum Disorders, and Persistent Developmental Delay. When evaluated with the sequence of SPECT, one HBOT, repeat SPECT I have found that these children's' brain blood flow pattern improves and predicts permanent improvement with additional HBOT similar to the boxers, divers, and patients with other diagnoses. This change in blood flow after one HBOT is clearly demonstrated in the 8 year old Persistent Developmental Delay/Autism patient I presented to Chairman Regula and which I present again today. His three dimensional brain scans are seen in the attached Case 1.

In addition, I have included two other cases, Cases 2 and 3. In all three cases you seen an improvement in brain blood flow and hence, metabolism, after one HBOT or a course of HBOT that was matched by an improvement in their autistic symptoms and behaviors. One child was able to be weaned from the powerful psychoactive drugs Ritalin and Prozac, and improve his emotional outbursts, autistic behavior, ability to play sports, and attend school. Another child whose autistic behavior was causing a significant emotional disturbance with inhibition of school performance in her six year old sister began to interact with her sister and family more normally with a resultant improvement in the sister and family unit. The third child experienced improvement in attention, understanding, sleep, vocabulary, inappropriate behavior, and emotional state.

Unfortunately, HBOT did not "cure" any of these patients but all of them improved remarkably. This is partly due to the great delay in application of this therapy and the fact that I didn't know Dr. Buttar when I treated these patients. Many physicians who treat with the Neubauer-Harch low-pressure hyperbaric protocol and some form of chelation have reported that the combination works better than either of the two therapies alone. I firmly believe that the combination of these two therapies will yield tremendous results in these patients, especially in those children who develop normally only to have a deterioration to autism by 2-5 years of age.

This approach is exactly what we will be following in our planned study through the IHMA Foundation's Treatment Registry. We're anxious to get started and can treat about 100 children for about $2 million. We are working to raise these funds now.

In the past 40 years a steadily accumulating body of animal and human research has led to the conclusion that the appropriate application of hyperbaric oxygen therapy to human and animal disease is a vast untapped inexpensive health resource with limitless potential. This is no surprise when one considers that the basis for all human life is oxygen, the vast majority of human illnesses have as their root pathophysiology an absence of blood flow and oxygen to tissues, and the restoration of oxygen in all of these conditions makes common sense. Thanks to this research and literature, it now also makes good scientific sense. Unfortunately, for a variety of political non-scientific reasons these simple facts have been lost on the medical profession often leading to the deplorable situation where patients have to become their own doctor in order to treat themselves with this life-saving and life-improving therapy.

To give you a few examples of the phenomenal potential of HBOT, I would like to quote from my testimony to Chairman Regula's House Appropriations Subcommittee on Labor, Health, Human Services, and Education last week, "...the scientific literature suggests that the most powerful drug for treating the vast majority of acute injuries to the human body is one pressurized dose of oxygen to saturate the body's tissues. That dose appears to have a generic effect regardless of the cause of the injury or its location in the body (Harch PG. Generic Inhibitory Drug Effect of Hyperbaric Oxygen Therapy (HBOT) on Reperfusion Injury (RI). Eur J Neurol, 2000;7(Suppl 3):150)." The benefits of HBOT in acute injury are most demonstrable and dramatic in the treatment of acute brain injuries, collectively the condition which is responsible for the vast majority of disability and human suffering and the condition for which doctors have been traditionally "brainwashed" that there is no treatment. For example, HBOT successfully resuscitated over half of a group of 65 babies in England born not breathing who failed standard resuscitation. (Today, sadly, the only way one can procure this therapy is if you are a high priced newborn thoroughbred racehorse in Kentucky or Florida whose racing future is jeopardized by birth injury from lack of oxygen and blood flow.)

In humans this application has never advanced beyond the original scientific report in 1963. Similarly, the great majority of 336 acute coma and cardiac arrest patients in China and 170 near-hanging patients in Northern France were successfully resuscitated with a single high pressure HBOT. HBOT delivered shortly after these brain insults seemed to work identically to the manner in which it has worked all of these years in the classic accepted application of HBOT, decompression illness of divers (Harch PG. Late Treatment of Decompression Illness and Use of SPECT Brain Imaging. In: Treatment of Decompression Illness, 45th UHMS Workshop, Eds. RE Moon, PJ Sheffield, Undersea and Hyperbaric Medical Society, Kensington, MD. 1996). Specifically, it treats the common major underlying problem called reperfusion injury, or the injury that occurs once blood flow and oxygen are restored.

Another exciting example of the use of HBOT is the combination of hyperbaric oxygen therapy with radiation therapy in the treatment of cancer patients. It has been shown the kill ratio of cancer cells by radiation is directly proportional to the oxygen content of the tissue. What more obvious common sense method to increase the oxygen content of tumors than by the administration of hyperbaric oxygen therapy? So thought researchers 35 years ago in New Orleans where some of this seminal work was performed. In just the past three years doctors in the Far East have delivered radiation therapy to patients with one of the most deadly of all cancers, brain cancer, within 15 minutes of exit from a hyperbaric oxygen chamber and shown an approximately 50% increase in survival. Marlo Thomas, the famous actress and benefactor of St. Jude's Medical Center in Memphis, Tennessee recounted to Chairman Regula immediately before my testimony last week how the researchers at St. Jude's are desperately seeking and hope to develop new therapies for the treatment of brain cancer in children with the addition of a new $80 million brain cancer center.

As I mentioned to Chairman Regula, that treatment of yesterday is here today; it is hyperbaric oxygen therapy. Interestingly, and seemingly paradoxically, this same treatment that is potentially so effective acutely in combination with radiation therapy is by far the most effective therapy for treatment of the late effects of radiation therapy. In now 67 of 74 worldwide studies on HBOT in the treatment of radiation injury to multiple different areas and organs of the human body the results were strongly positive (Feldmeier JJ, Hampson NB. A Systematic Review of the Literature Reporting the Application of Hyperbaric Oxygen Prevention and Treatment of Delayed Radiation Injuries; An Evidence Based Approach. Undersea and Hyper Med, 2002;29(1):4-30.

While we have evidence for the great potential of HBOT in acute injury my concern today is for the millions of individuals in the United States and hundreds of millions of individuals worldwide who suffer from chronic brain injury of all types. Given the information above about the nature of acute brain injury, namely, the deprivation of oxygen and blood flow, and the common underlying process of secondary injury in so many of these conditions, it is no surprise that many chronic conditions, especially of the brain, are characterized by low oxygenation and blood flow. In 1990 I realized that we could treat this chronic injury by discovering that a lower dose of HBOT pioneered in South Florida by Dr. Richard Neubauer in stroke and multiple sclerosis patients could be successfully applied to, once again, the classic accepted condition for HBOT, decompression illness of divers.

I found that divers who had failed standard United States Navy HBOT or divers who presented weeks to months after their diving accident with decompression illness of the brain could be permanently improved neurologically, cognitively, and emotionally and return to a functional high quality life. My partners, Drs. Keith Van Meter and Sheldon Gottlieb, simultaneously were proving this in brain injured boxers. With these two doctors I then extended the findings in divers to patients with now over 50 different neurological conditions using SPECT brain blood flow imaging before and after a single HBOT to predict which patients had injured brain tissue that could respond to a course of HBOT.

This pattern of response first seen in a stroke patient of Dr. Neubauer's and then in the boxers and divers was yet another generic response to HBOT that I identified in the vast majority of the fifty additional diagnoses, including the first cerebral palsy case in North America (Harch PG, Gottlieb SF, Staab P, Van Meter KW. HMPAO SPECT Brain Imaging and Low Pressure HBOT in the Diagnosis and Treatment of Chronic Traumatic, Ischemic, Hypoxic, and Anoxic Encephalopathies. Undersea and Hyper Med, 1994;21(Suppl):30. In other words, if one HBOT could change the pattern of brain blood flow in a neurologically abnormal patient to a more normal pattern, this was evidence that that injured brain could positively and permanently respond to a course of HBOT.

In summary, Chairman Burton, we have a treatment, right now, for autism, that combines these two proven therapies. It produces demonstrable results as you have seen today. We also have a treatment for acute and chronic brain injury that is so simple, giving oxygen, specifically hyperbaric oxygen, as to be astounding that is not more universally applied in the field of medicine. Given the research and experience to date and its potential application to autism I do not hesitate to tell you that HBOT will revolutionize the treatment of brain injury in the world.

Thank you for this opportunity.

Paul Harch, M.D., President
International Hyperbaric Medical Association Foundation

Case Presentation #1

Autism & Persistent Developmental Delay (PDD)

- 7 year old male who is repeating kindergarten.
  - * Born one week overdue and a difficult labor, becoming "stuck" in the birth canal and requiring forceps extraction.
  - * Global developmental delay. Patient on Ritalin and Prozac.
- Main problems included poor enunciation, limited vocabulary, short, nearly unintelligible sentences, no coordination, 2 year cognitive delay, attention deficit, emotional outbursts, autistic behavior, and drooling.
- Scan 1: Baseline scan shows decreased flow, to the frontal lobes and both temporal lobes, especially the left.
- Scan 2: 1 HBOT treatment shows recoverable tissue & improvement to both temporal lobes.
- Patient received 40 HBOTs and weaned from Ritalin and Prozac.
  - * Drooling gone, speech and cognition improved.
  - * Dad stated that the attention deficit was "1000% improved and emotional outbursts and autistic tendencies 100,000%" improved.
- Patient received another 25 HBOT treatments over the next year and continued to globally improve. He now speaks in full sentences and very active in sports for the first time in his life.
  - * He continues to be medication free.

Case Presentation #1

Autism & Persistent Developmental Delay (PDD)

7 y. male

Baseline

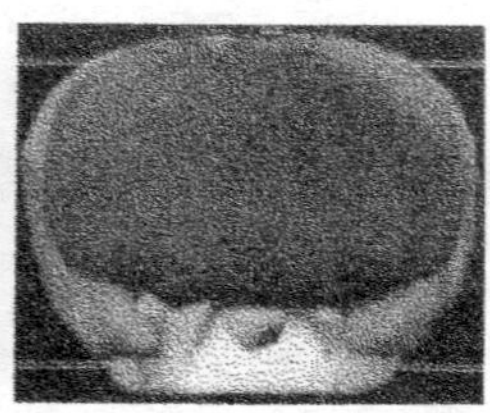

1 HBOT

Diagnostic showing recoverable brain tissue

May 6, 2004 Government Oversight Committee
Copyright Retained
Paul G. Harch, M.D. 2004

Case Presentation #2

Autism

- Two ½ year old girl, C-section birth, to mother whose pregnancy was complicated by freon exposure x 2, asthma, bronchitis, nausea, vomiting, dehydration with hospital admission in third trimester.
  - * Child had severe reflux with minimal weight gain first two months.
  - * Abnormal social interaction and laugh at 3 months.
  - * MRI normal, abnormal EEG
- Problems: No communication, minimal emotional development, dd/inappropriate behavior, hypotonia
- First SPECT: Bilateral temporal and frontal lobe abnormalities
- SPECT after 1 HBOT and course of HBOT: Improved
- HBOT: Three month course
  - * Improved: Self feeding, eye contact, tone, attention/interaction; increased activity, appetite and weight gain, stopped biting people, calmer. Very loving, improved relationship with 6 year old sister that improved sister's emotional disturbance caused by the patient's autism—beneficial effect on entire family.

Case Presentation #2

Autism

2 ½ y. female

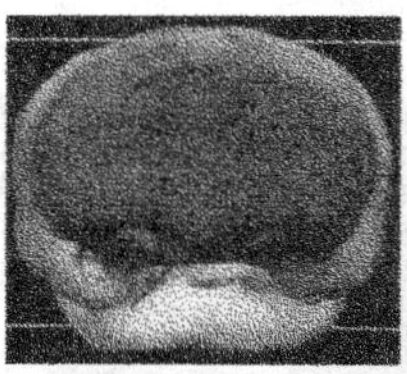

Baseline

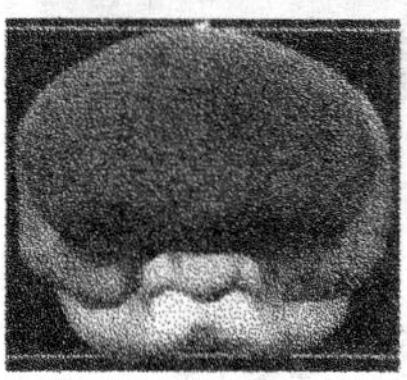

40 HBOT

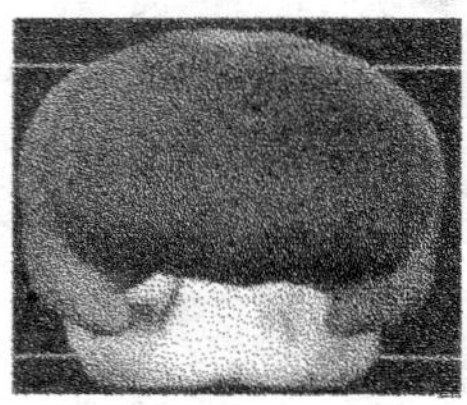

1 HBOT

Diagnostic showing recoverable brain tissue

May 6, 2004 Government Oversight Committee
Copyright Retained
Paul G. Harch, M.D. 2004

Case Presentation #3

Autism

- Eight year old girl. Normal pregnancy and delivery.
  - Bottle-fed, aspiration in hospital with cyanosis. Resuscitation without intubation.
  - Hospitalized for 5 days.
- 4 months old: Incoordination, poor eye movement, blank stare, delayed motor.
  - Extensive evaluation for two years
- Problems: Minimal speech, limited understanding, global motor delay, abnormal gait, inability to sleep, autistic behaviors.
  - MRI: microcephaly.
  - Underwent multiple treatments, including secretin, ongoing chelation
- First SPECT: Abnormal temporal and frontal lobes, especially left side
- SPECT after 1 HBOT and course of HBOT: Improved
- HBOT: Three blocks of treatment over two years.
  - Improved attention span, vocabulary, communication, understanding, behavior, calmer, follows commands. Previously needed four sleeping pills at night, now one and sleeps most of the night.

Case Presentation #3

Autism

8 y. female

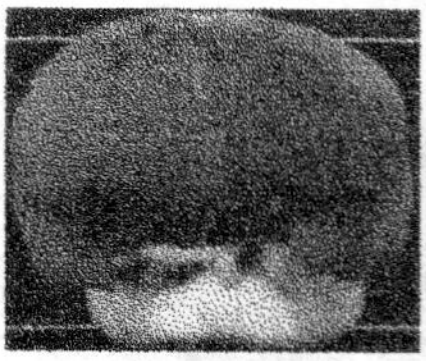

Baseline

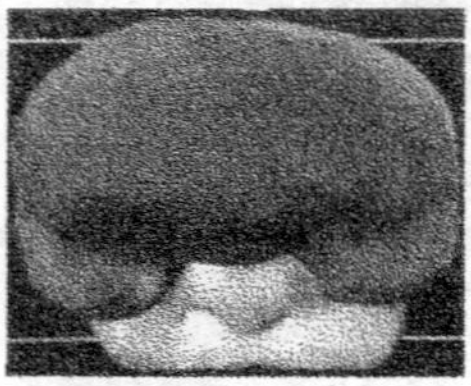

1 HBOT

Diagnostic showing recoverable brain tissue

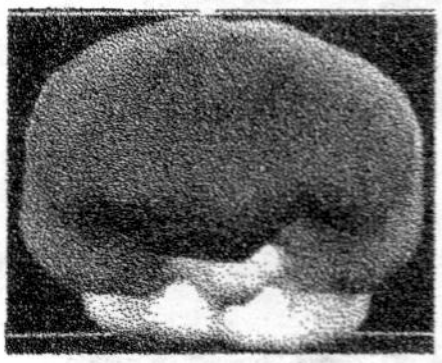

40 HBOT

Mr. BURTON. Dr. Stoller.

Dr. STOLLER. Chairman Burton and distinguished member of the subcommittee, thank you for this opportunity to speak with you today.

Ignoring hyperbaric medicine has come at a great societal cost. The past is the past. I am here with one of my patients, 10-year old Augusta Skoog, who began life as an 11-week preemie with the most severe grade of intraventricular bleed in her brain. She has the diagnosis of cerebral palsy but began her Hyperbaric Oxygen Therapy last year. It is now 2004, and we can document either by spec scan or neurocognitive evaluations concrete evidence of dramatic improvements children with brain injuries can make if they can receive treatment with Hyperbaric Oxygen Therapy.

These neurocognitive changes are, in many cases, quasi miraculous, given the short time required to manifest these permanent improvements. Every published research study that has looked at the efficacy of using Hyperbaric Oxygen Therapy to treat children with cerebral palsy has found significant levels of improvement. The most recent study published in the United States was in the U.S. Army Medical Journal in 2002.

Brain injuries that are considered irreversible and incurable, such as the case of fetal alcohol syndrome now being treated in New Mexico, do respond to Hyperbaric Oxygen Therapy, respond immediately, and can now be documented. Fetal alcohol syndrome, for example, is one of the leading causes of mental retardation in this country.

The government and Medicaid are the insurers of last resort for most of these children, and the cost is astronomical. The CDC reports that the overall economic cost for just one child with cerebral palsy is $40 million over their lifetime.

Yes, the past is the past. Now there is a therapy for brain injury, replete with documentation that can return people to work, return them to school, and give them a life worth living, as well as drastically reducing government costs for these brain injuries. So can these children get treated with Hyperbaric Oxygen Therapy? After all, Medicaid's EPSDT statute says that any treatment that either corrects or ameliorates, be it a covered benefit of a State plan or not, shall not be denied a handicapped child. However, most States ignore this aspect of Medicaid law and force families to take legal avenues to seek reimbursement. This week, Augusta was denied for the third time by New Mexico Medicaid from getting Hyperbaric Oxygen Therapy, despite both her pediatrician and neurologist requesting it for her.

Medicaid law, the science of Hyperbaric Oxygen Therapy, and prudent economics are all present behind this therapy. It is time for it to be made known and available to all brain-injured children, even if it requires Congress to remind State Medicaid programs of their obligation in regard to brain injury and hyperbaric therapy.

It is important to support evidence-based medical programs such as the Oklahoma University Center of Autism. It is important to mandate that State Medicaid programs do literally obey the law. It is important to help bring Hyperbaric Oxygen Therapy to the forefront if for no other reason than to save everyone's precious health care dollars.

There is a pernicious catch–22 at work. As most State Medicaid agencies have decided their reimbursement policies for Hyperbaric Oxygen Therapy should be modeled after Medicare policy but the Medicare policy on Hyperbaric Oxygen Therapy is formulated based on research and data collected on people age 65 and older, CMS will reject petitions made to it for new cases that are not relevant to this population; and, therefore, Hyperbaric Oxygen Therapy for brain-injured children does not have any opportunity to be covered no matter how much research is presented. That is simply the way the system operates at the moment.

How can a Medicaid HBOT policy for children truly provide services for children if its plan is based on a government model that is not designed for children? It makes no financial sense to use the Medicare model on which to base health care decisions for children, particularly brain-injured children.

Thank you very much.

Mr. BURTON. Thank you, Dr. Stoller. I presume that we have a detailed statement.

Dr. STOLLER. Yes. I provided testimony. The graphs of Augusta's incredible and dramatic neurocognitive changes are documented in the testimony, as well as the fetal alcohol syndrome case I was talking about.

Mr. BURTON. We just want to have as much information as possible so we can submit it in the right way.

[The prepared statement of Dr. Stoller follows:]

Hyperbaric Medicine and Brain Injured Children

Prepared for the Committee on Government Reform for the May 6th, 2004 Hearing (Autism Spectrum Disorders: An Update of Federal Government Initiatives and Revolutionary New Treatment of Neurodevelopmental Diseases)

By: Kenneth Stoller, M.D., F.A.A.P.
Chairman of the Pediatrics Committee, IHMA Foundation
Clinical Assistant Professor, University of NM, School of Medicine, Dept of Pediatrics
Diplomat, American Board of Hyperbaric Medicine
Diplomat, American Board of Pediatrics

Hyperbaric Medicine has been repairing brain injuries for 30 years, but neither academia nor the governmental insurance complex took a look at it because everyone "knew" that it was not possible.

Hyperbaric oxygen therapy (HBOT) involves the delivery of oxygen in a pressurized environment created by a chamber. The pressure serves to saturate the tissues of the body, not only the hemoglobin in the blood, but the plasma, lymph and cerebral spinal fluid, all of which go many places that hemoglobin cannot reach, especially in cases of traumatic injury.

Vol. 44 / No. 37 MMWR 697

Birth Defects and Cerebral Palsy — Continued

TABLE 2. Incidence rate and estimated economic costs* of cerebral palsy and 17 of the most clinically important birth defects, by condition and type of cost — United States, 1992

Condition	Incidence rate†	Direct costs: Medical§ (millions)	Direct costs: Nonmedical¶ (millions)	Indirect costs** (millions)	Total costs†† (millions)	Cost per new case (thousands)
Nervous system						
Cerebral palsy**	12.3	$ 852	$445	$1,120	$2,428	$503
Spina bifida	4.2	$ 205	$ 43	$ 241	$ 489	$294
Cardiovascular						
Truncus arteriosus	1.1	$ 109	$ <1	$ 101	$ 210	$505
Single ventricle	1.3	$ 62	$ <1	$ 110	$ 173	$344
Transposition/ Double outlet right ventricle	4.8	$ 166	$ 4	$ 344	$ 515	$267
Tetralogy of fallot	3.5	$ 185	$ 4	$ 171	$ 360	$262
Alimentary tract						
Tracheo-esophageal fistula**	2.9	$ 62	—	$ 103	$ 165	$145

Figure (1) was taken from a 1995 CDC report showing the yearly cost of a child with Cerebral Palsy is $503K

Children with neurological injuries cost, on average, 2.1 times as much to educate as a non-injured child. There are 6.548 million Individuals with Disabilities Education Act (IDEA) children in the nation, who are costing the state's educational system $47 billion, for a total of $55.7 billion. On average, nationally, they cost $8,510 more per year to educate than a "normal" child. Many cannot learn due to their injuries. Hyperbaric oxygen therapy (HBOT) would cost an average, one time expenditure of between $7,000 and $14,000 for most children treated long after the injury, the cost of educating them for a year or two. The effects would be permanent and last throughout their lifetime. For many of these children, if they had been treated immediately upon injury, the costs drop to often less than $1,000.

Many of these children have neurological injuries that affect their motor skills, learning, speech, etc. They are children injured in birth trauma, accidents, child abuse, fetal alcohol syndrome, maternal drug use, or other such events. HBOT has effectively recovered and rebuilt brain tissue through reactivation of stunned tissue, revascularization and, possibly, stimulation of stems cells in the brain to repair existing neural pathways and grow new ones. In 1992, Rockswold(GL) reported the most exhaustive, rigorous, and important study in acute Traumatic Brain Injury (TBI). Conducted from 1983 to 1989 the study enrolled 168 patients with Glasgow Coma Scale (GCS) of 9 or less in a randomized prospective controlled trial (RPCT). Overall mortality was significantly reduced 50% in the HBOT group (60% in the group with increased ICP).

In 2001, Rockwold(SB), on a group of severe TBI patients similar to those in the 1992 study found that HBOT improved the cerebral metabolic rate for oxygen and decreased CSF lactate (a marker of damaged brain cells), and reduced ICP. These author's showed HBOT's ability to recouple blood flow with metabolism.

> The neurosurgeon authors of the Rockswold study conclude that "HBOT should be initiated as soon as possible after acute severe traumatic brain injury." (*Results of a prospective randomized trial for treatment of severely brain injured patients with hyperbaric oxygen. Authors: Rockswold GL , et al Division of Neurosurgery, Hennepin County Medical Center, Minneapolis, Minnesota. J Neurosurg 1992 Jun;76(6):929-34. Effects of hyperbaric oxygenation therapy on cerebral metabolism and intracranial pressure in severely brain injured patients.* Authors: Rockswold SB, Rockswold GL et al J Neurosurg *March 2001; 94:403-411).*

Follow children with brain injuries into adulthood and you may discover that many wind up in prison, on welfare, Social Security Disability, in long-term care facilities at state or insurance company expense or become a drain on the system in some other fashion. I served as the pediatrician of the Santa Fe County Youth Development Program for several years and I know first hand that many of these children suffer from a neurological injury incurred prior to incarceration. Many of these children are suffering Mental Retardation or Developmental Disabilities, when they grow to adulthood, cost, on average, $43,000 per year in group home or institutional settings. HBOT has demonstrated that nearly all of these children can be helped, including many with genetic disorders, and many, many, can lead full, normal and productive lives. This is something current medical practices cannot provide for most of them.

The old concept of cerebral palsy being a "static insult" is no longer tenable. It is now recognized in neurology that deterioration due to brain damage at birth may take place over 28 years. (*St Hilaire MHS, Burke RE, Bressman SB, Brin MF, Fahn S. Delayed-onset dystonia due to perinatal or early childhood asphyxia. Neurology 1991;41:216-222.*) This mirrors the adult situation (*Burke RE, Fahn S, Gold AP. Delayed-onset dystonia in patients with "static" encephalopathy. J Neurol Neurosurg Psychiatry 1980;43:789-797.*) Further over the last decade stem or progenitor cells have been found in the adult brain and they can result in neural regeneration. (*Steindler DA, Pincus DW. Stem cells and neuropoesis in the adult human brain. Lancet 2002;359:1047-54*). This recovery process is oxygen dependent and on first principles much more likely to take place in a growing child than an adult. There is now conclusive evidence from altitude studies that the capillary density even in the adult mammalian brain can be increased. (*Harik SI, Behmand RA, LaManna JC. Hypoxia increases glucose transport at the blood-brain barrier. J Appl Physiol 1994;77:896-901*).

Every published research study that has looked at the efficacy of using HBOT to treat children with cerebral palsy has found significant levels of improvement; the most recent study was published in the US Army Medical Journal in 2002, "Adjunctive HBO Treatment of Children with Cerebral Anoxic Injury" by Waalkes et al. [4]

Neurologists have promoted the concept of the ischemic penumbra[1] for many years and both magnetic resonance imaging of children with brain injuries and pathological studies[2] have shown that the changes are essentially the same as adults. They range from edema, which is treatable, to cystic degeneration, which is not. Stem cells have been demonstrated in the adult brain[3] and so must obviously be present during childhood.

Parents have been in the vanguard of the efforts to provide oxygen treatment for children with cerebral palsy in the UK and North America and they actually prompted the funding by the Canadian government of the infamous Quebec/McGill University study. Parents also prompted the study by the US Army[4] which has confirmed the benefit found in the McGill study. The study conducted at McGill University[5] published in the Lancet became infamous because the authors used compressed-air at 1.3 atmospheres absolute (ata) for one arm of the study mistakenly believing that such an air pressure could be regarded as a placebo. This was corrected in the Lancet review process and the terms placebo and controlled were not allowed to be used in the paper. Compressed air at 1.3 ata raises the plasma oxygen tension by almost 50% and that alone was enough for the children with cerebral palsy in that group as well as the treatment arm to show significant gains. Everyone agreed that both groups improved significantly. As a matter of fact none of these children had ever had this type of rapid improvement before. Keep in mind they only received a total of 4O HBOT treatments.

The bottom line is that at an age where one did not expect any dramatic changes, the children in studies conducted by Dr. Marois showed "many tremendous functional improvements."[6] "Some children started to walk, to speak, or to sit for the first time in their lives. The motor changes that were seen and measured with GMFM,[7] were greater, more generalized, and were obtained in a shorter period of time than most of the improvements found in any other studies of recognized conventional therapies in the treatment of children with CP."

The protocol of treating a minimum of 40 times at 1.5 ATA for non-acute brain injury, is a direct outgrowth of 20 years clinical experience with brain injury of Dr. RA Neubauer in Florida (1970-1990), the published reports of Drs. RA Neubauer and SF Gottlieb, the initial experience of Van Meter and Gottlieb with boxers in New Orleans 1989, and the clinical experience of Harch from 1990-present that was refined to its present state in the prospective trial of chronic brain injury, SPECT, and HBOT by Harch and Gottlieb 1993-9 that tested blocks of 40 HBOT's. At the start of the investigation in 1992 and 1993 Harch and Gottlieb applied HBOT to the first cerebral palsy child in North America (ref #13) The experience in New Orleans was stimulated by the observation that patients with neurological conditions treated with standard HBOT for chronic wound problems experienced concomitant improvement in their neurological problems.

In 1989, Drs. RA Neubauer and SF Gottlieb used a variation of normal SPECT imaging on a 60 year old woman who had experienced a stroke 14 years previously. They performed two consecutive SPECT brain scans with a single exposure to low pressure HBO immediately before the scan. When they compared the after-oxygen scan with the before-oxygen scan they noticed that the after-oxygen scan had a greater uptake of the radioactive tracer, i.e. improved blood flow, and thereby, a decrease in the brain injury. After 60 HBO treatments they were able to recover a fair amount of neurological function in this patient even though the therapy was started 14 years after her stroke. Drs. Neubauer and Gottlieb published this report and two additional cases of near drowning and natural gas poisoning.[8,9,10]

Subsequently, Drs. Harch and Van Meter performed the same sequence of SPECT scan/HBO therapy/SPECT scan on commercial divers with brain DCS and obtained results similar to those of Neubauer and Gottlieb.[11,12,13]

This growing body of prospective experience provided the explanation for the phenomena described earlier where patients with neurological problems who were being treated for non-neurological reasons experienced gratuitous neurological improvement as their hyperbaric treatment progressed.

Commercial divers with decompression sickness of the brain or spinal cord were flown in comatose and/or paralyzed from the oil and gas fields of the Gulf of Mexico. The recoveries of these injured divers showed improvement in neurological levels far exceeded published reports and current expectations. The notable improvement was due to a protocol that treated beyond the medical standard of a few hyperbaric oxygen therapy treatments. Some patients required as many as 100 treatments before reaching a clinical plateau.

Standard diving medicine principles suggest that decompression sickness (DCS) involves bubble formation in the circulatory system thereby interfering with the necessary continuous supply of oxygen and nutrients to the nerve cells in one or more areas of the brain or spinal cord. Minutes to hours after the onset of decompression illness, tissue damage continues to develop because of persistent occlusion of blood vessels by bubbles or secondary damage to the blood vessel caused by passage of the bubbles. This secondary damage is virtually identical to the pathological processes occurring during acute stroke after the blood clot has been dissolved and circulation restored. Even after the initial trauma to the brain and the initial course of therapy, there may be residual damage to the nerve cells. The initial hyperbaric oxygenation (HBO) treatments are thought to help remove bubbles from the circulatory system of the brain or spinal cord if the patient is being treated in the acute phase of DCS. In 1996 Harch argued that early HBO was also treating the acute aforementioned secondary damage called reperfusion injury, and the downstream tissue damage resulting from interrupted blood flow and oxygen delivery (Harch PG. Late treatment of decompression illness and use of SPECT brain imaging. 45th Undersea and Hyperbaric Medical Society Workshop, Treatment of Decompression Illness, eds. RE Moon, PJ Sheffield. June 18-19, 1995, Palm Beach, Florida. Undersea and Hyperbaric Medical Society, Kensington, MD. 1996) Repetitive hyperbaric oxygen treatments tend to result in improving the function of tissues and nerves that show residual damage resulting from the trauma. The progressive improvement in nerve function seen by Harch and Van Meter in DCS cases is due to the HBO treatment protocols they have used over the last couple of decades (Harch PG. Vide supra. Van Meter KW, article in 45th UHMS Workshop).

In a paper titled "Analysis of the results of a randomized study of hyperbaric oxygen therapy in a treatment of children with cerebral palsy: Placebo or physiological effect?" by Dr. Pierre Marois and Dr. Michel Vanasse (both who were part of the research team to conduct the McGill study), state, "we can therefore establish that the hyperbaric therapy resulted in functional improvements more rapidly and more generalized than conventional treatment. If we accept that the improvement observed in the children having received HBO therapy is due to a placebo, must we then conclude the improvements resulting from the 6-8 months of intensive physical therapy were also due to placebo because the results were identical?" In the same article they write, "another interesting and, in our opinion, very important element that was highlighted by our research was that the improvements persisted at least three months post treatment. The children were systematically re-evaluated three months later and we were able to document beyond doubt the persistence of the gains observed after 40 hyperbaric treatments. To our knowledge, no scientific proof exists confirming the persistence of a placebo for that period of time."

On May 2, 2002 Dr. Paul G. Harch was invited and presented evidence for a restorative effect of low pressure HBOT on chronic brain injury before the Subcommittee on Labor, Health, Human Services, and Education of the House of Representatives Appropriations Committee. The testimony consisted of functional brain imaging (SPECT) documentation of improvements in brain blood flow in 15 patients with a variety of chronic brain injuries.
The diversity of cases in the testimony and the uniform results using a low pressure protocol of HBOT strongly suggest a generic effect of HBOT on the chronically injured brain. The impressive brain scans demonstrate the power of this treatment modality.

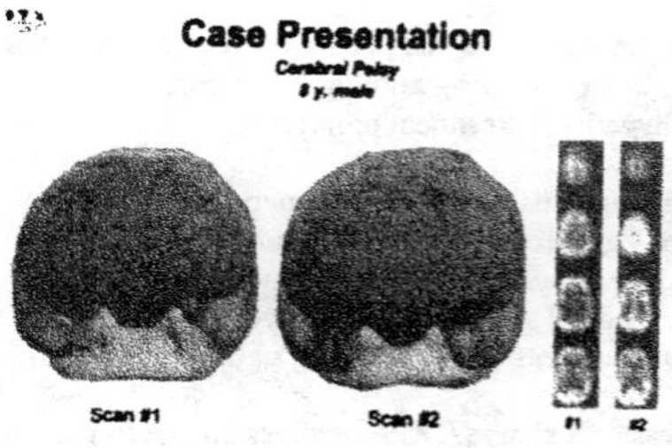

Figure (2) SPECT scan of an eight year old boy with cerebral palsy before and after HBOT as presented by Paul Harch, M.D at a 2002 House of Representatives Appropriations Committee.

It is clear from authoritative medical literature that that SPECT brain blood flow imaging is a respected and scientifically valid measurement of the changes taking place when HBOT is administered to a brain injured child. It is a picture of the biological changes that take place under hyperbaric conditions.

ıe Case of Augusta

ıave brought with me one of my patients – ten year old Augusta Skoog. Augusta was born 11 weeks emature –the product of a precipitous delivery and had an intraventricular hemorrhage at birth from the ıuma on her head due to the pressures exerted in the birth canal. She was officially diagnosed with right astic hemiplegia, hearing impairment, and developmental delay at one year and seven months of age. ıgusta was nine years old when we were introduced. Her neurocognitive functions were determined by a mputerized neurocognitive test battery (*IMPACT*) developed originally to evaluate sports concussions at ɛ University of Pittsburgh.[14,15] This is the first time this test has been used to evaluate changes in urocognitive function from HBOT in a child with cerebral palsy.

ıe computer administered test battery consists of seven individual test modules that measure aspects of gnitive functioning including attention, memory, reaction time, and processing speed.

ble 1. Neuropsychological Test Modules of the *IMPACT* test.

st Module	Ability Area
ɔrd Discrimination	Attentional processes, verbal recognition
mbol Memory	Visual working memory, visual processing speed
quential Digit Tracking	Sustained attention, reaction time
sual Span	Visual attention, immediate memory
mbol-Matching	Visual processing speed, learning and memory
ılour Click	Focused attention, response inhibition, reaction time
ree Letters	Working memory, visual-motor response speed

ısults from above tests are computed into overall Memory, Reaction Time, and Processing Speed composite scores.

n October 9th of 2003, Augusta completed 40 hyperbaric oxygen treatments and before and after results ı her testing are compared. Her Verbal Memory composite score went from 62% (7/24/03) to 82% - (a ›% improvement). Half way through this first set of ɛatments (8/25/03), her OT (occupational therapist) ʼaluation noted that "use of both sides of the body gether and separately in a smooth coordinated fashion is ıproving by over 40% on a consistent basis." "Trunk tation is evidenced at 50% improvement compared to ıe year ago."

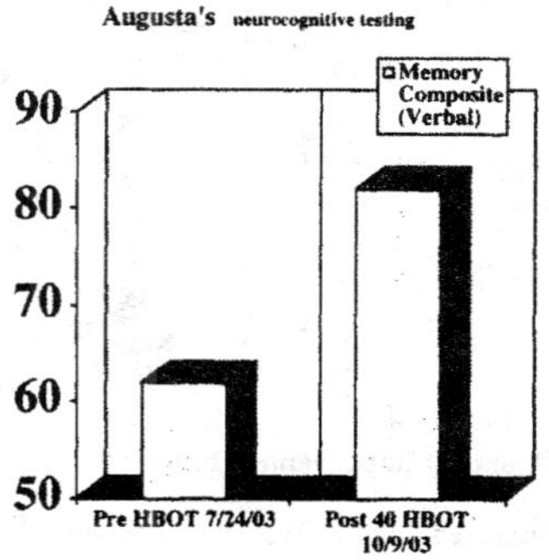

Figure (3) Improvement in Verbal Memory after 40 HBO treatments. *(y axis score developed fr the clinical research of Drs. Lovell and Collins at the University of Pittsburgh Center for Sports Medicine)*

On October 13, 2003, her PT (physical therapist) wrote, "Augusta's ability to perform activities in a symmetrical way has improved from 50 to 70% (from 7/25/03). Her bilateral skills have improved 25% (from 7/25/03). Endurance improved by 100%."

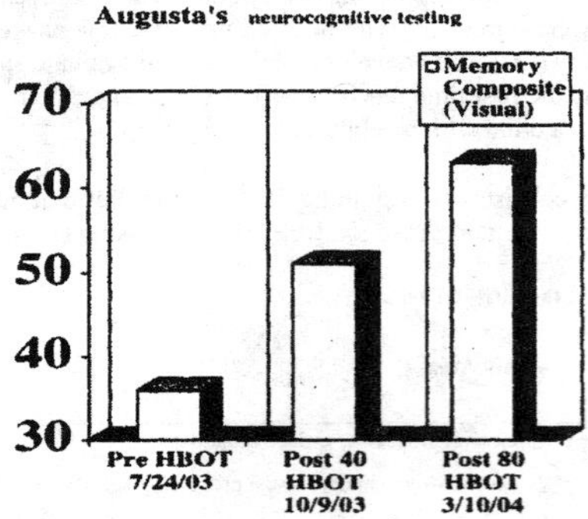

Figure (4) Improvement in Visual Memory after 40 HBO treatments, and 80 HBOT

In March of 2004, Augusta completed her second set of 40 treatments with hyperbaric oxygen and Figure (4) shows the improvement in Augusta's Visual Memory over the course of two blocks of 40 HBO treatments – a 75% improvement from her pre-HBOT score on 7/24/03.

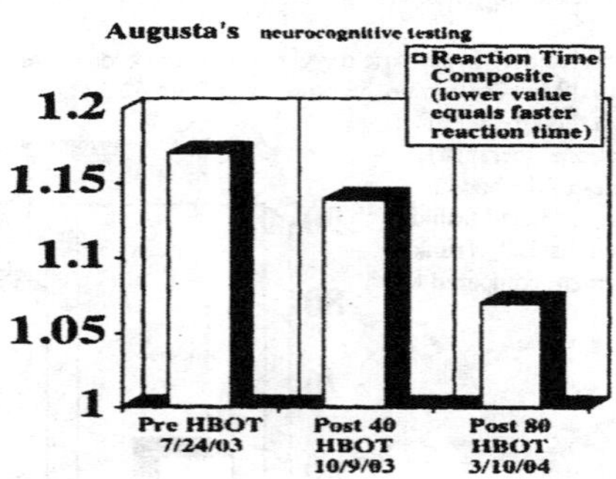

Figure (5) Improvement in Reaction Time after 40 HBO treatments, and 80 HBOT

While still impaired, Figure (5) shows consistent improvement in Reaction Time over the course of Augusta's HBOT sets. These stellar results are representative of what hyperbaric oxygenation can do for a brain injured child. Now, every brain injury is unique unto itself, and results of HBOT vary from patient to patient influenced by a myriad of factors such as age therapy is initiated the extent of the injury, nutritional status, etc. In Augusta's case, damage resulted from a single traumatic event, but many neonates and infants can have multiple and prolonged bouts of oxygen deprivation due to prematurity and/or infection. Although each case is different in the extent and type of damage, using hyperbaric oxygenation to preserve or restore function after brain injury should be considered as fundamental as establishing an airway. Least we forget, the object of intervention in head injury is to maintain an adequate level of oxygen to the brain; although, for some reason this is apparently not obvious.

Figure (6) Ten year old Augusta with fellow patients inside the hyperbaric chamber in Santa Fe.

The Case of Slava

Slava was found abandoned and wandering a Rustov, Russia train station as a toddler. When brought to the USA by his adoptive mother he was diagnosed with Fetal Alcohol Syndrome (FAS). Slava, now in his mid teens, has just begun his HBOT but already has shown significant neurocognitive gains as documented by the IMPACT test.

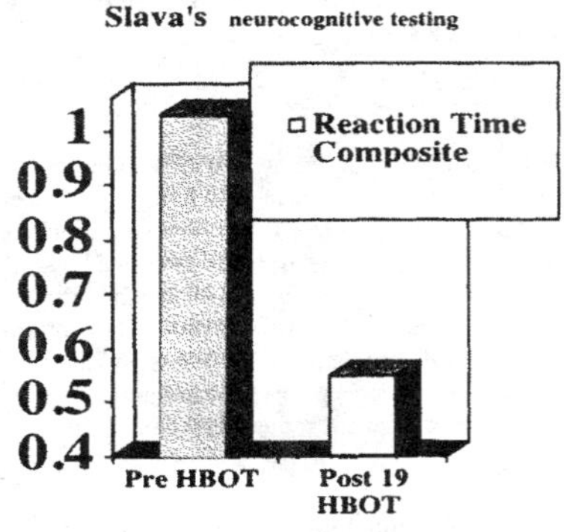

Figure (7) Improvement in Reaction Time after 19 HBO treatments (4/23/04), an improvement of 53%.

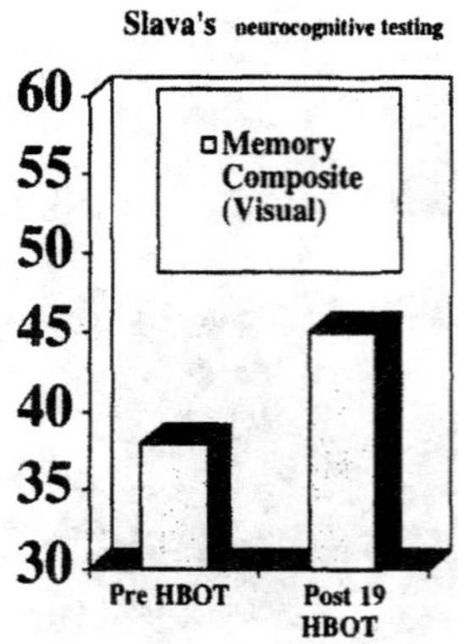

Figure (8) improvement in Visual Memory after 19 HBO treatments (4/23/04), an 18% increase in performance.

The data/documentation that can be generated using a tool, such as the IMPACT neurocognitive evaluation system, demonstrates not only the remarkable improvement children such as Slava and Augusta can make with HBOT, but shows that these children can act as their own controls for the purpose of evaluating the efficacy and effectiveness of HBOT for brain injured children.

Fetal Alcohol Syndrome is one of the leading causes of mental retardation and birth defects in this country. This syndrome is considered irreversible and there is no treatment for it. Slava is the first child with FAS to be getting a therapy that is drastically improving his neurocognitive abilities and he is having these dramatic changes documented as Figure 7 & 8 attest.

Oxygen: An Orphan Drug

Why is there such resistance to giving more oxygen under hyperbaric conditions, not only in the new or "controversial" areas such as neuro-rehabilitation, but also in a wide variety of diseases where it could save lives and improve the outcome of treatment? The principle reason is the current "culture" of medicine will not embrace a therapy that is neither taught in medical school nor promoted by a big pharmaceutical house. There are also those that have a vested interest in protecting an agenda who have had great influence on suppressing HBOT to the point of misrepresentation and prevarication. The bottom line is that the current generation of teachers at our medical schools do not themselves understand the importance of barometric pressure in oxygen delivery. If such fundamental concepts as pressure and tissue oxygenation are not grasped properly before a doctor qualifies or matriculates, then it is almost impossible for them to be taught later.

HBOT was first defined as a drug in 1977 by Gottlieb. Unfortunately, this critical definition has been long forgotten and substitute definitions have mischaracterized HBOT as a therapy for "certain recalcitrant, expensive, or otherwise hopeless medical problems." In 1999, the drug definition of HBOT was refined and restated as the use of greater than atmospheric pressure oxygen as a drug to treat basic pathophysiologic processes and their diseases. For the first time, this definition permitted an understanding of how all the conditions, which HBOT can help treat, can be connected as cohesive sets where a common pathophysiology is shared. Yet, medical students are taught little about oxygen except that it can be toxic in excess. Oxygen is toxic when given in excessive amounts for too long, but this is only relevant to divers. We know more about the actions of oxygen and the safe limits of its delivery than we do about any drug.

Oxygen has been extensively used in military and commercial diving for over sixty years and millions of hours of oxygen breathing have been completed underwater since the midget submarine charioteers bravely attacked ships in the Second World War. Similarly, pure oxygen breathing is necessary in military aircraft and for extra vehicular activity (EVA) in the space program. Although these activities have involved thousands of scientists and engineers, very few doctors have been involved, and so it should be no surprise that most physicians know very little about hyperbaric conditions and the need for the higher dosages of oxygen made possible at increased atmospheric pressure. But aren't physicians monitoring oxygen levels routinely in clinical practice? No, they measure the oxygenation of hemoglobin (the molecule that carries oxygen within the red blood cells). This value gives no direct indication of the amount of oxygen reaching the body's tissues. So, in major conditions, such as with heart attacks or strokes, the amount of oxygen being carried by the blood may be normal but the tissues of the heart or brain are dying of hypoxia – lack of oxygen, yet third party payers and their physician advisors often do not see HBOT as a medical necessity.

How does a therapy become a Medical Necessity?

How do Medicaid, Medicare and other third party payers decide what diagnoses are considered covered expenses and what diagnoses are considered investigational and does that determine whether a therapy is or isn't a medical necessity? What specific standard is applied to all diagnoses?

Both the 1999 Tec Assessment from BlueCross/BlueShield (BCBS) and the Undersea Hyperbaric Medical Society (UHMS) make it quite clear that HBOT is approved and reimbursed for conditions that lack any blinded, randomized controlled clinical trials. The UHMS also admitted that there exist no definitive criteria to determine what is approved and what is unapproved. It is Blue Cross Blue Shield's position that HBOT continues to be used and reimbursed for specific diagnoses despite the lack of controlled studies. Medicare, Medicaid and all other third party payers readily reimburse for those "experimental" and "investigational" applications of HBOT such as decompression sickness and air embolism.
Most of the medical therapies we offer children with neurological injuries do not meet the criteria of peer-reviewed double blind controlled studies published in authoritative journals to support their use with certainty for a particular diagnosis. For example, a recent article in the New England Journal of Medicine (NEJM) titled "Phenobarbital Compared with Phenytoin for the Treatment of Neonatal Seizures" states that both of the above mentioned drugs are ineffective in treating seizures in neonates and that phenobarbital may have negative effects on the developing brain and phenytoin can be toxic to heart tissue. Yet both these drugs are a covered "benefit" across the United States by all insurance carriers for neonates having seizures. Most seizure medications for the pediatric population lack any studies to support their use.

As a matter of fact there are few peer-reviewed double blind controlled studies published in authoritative journals for any drug given to the pediatric population.

Almost every drug given to a child is an off-label use of a drug that has Federal Drug Administration (FDA) approval for adults. According to the American Academy of Pediatrics only a small fraction of all drugs marketed in the United States has been studied in pediatric patients, and a majority of marketed drugs are not labeled, or are insufficiently labeled, for use in pediatric patients (Committee on Drugs, American Academy of Pediatrics, Guidelines for Ethical Conduct of Studies to Evaluate Drugs in Pediatric Populations, Pediatrics, 95(2);286-294, 1995.)

Hyperbaric chambers are a FDA approved and regulated medical device, and medical grade oxygen is a FDA approved and regulated drug. It is also a well established fact that both Medicare and Medicaid reimburse for both medical grade oxygen and for HBOT. Furthermore, all insurance plans including Medicaid will reimburse for drugs or therapies given to children even though those drugs or therapies are "off-label." What does it mean that a drug or device is used "off-label"?

When a drug or device is approved for marketing by the FDA it has to state a list of indications of use. The list would include what diagnoses this drug or device would be used to treat. When the drug or device is used for a particular diagnosis that does not appear on the original list then for that indication it is considered "off-label". (Device Labeling Guidance, FDA Guidance Doc. No. G-91, pt. III May 8, 1991) Off-label uses are neither risky nor investigational. The off-label designation by the FDA is simply a term they use to mean they are silent on the indicated use. The off-label use of a drug or medical device may be less risky than the approved indications. All drugs and devices contain inherent risks. Off-label simply means it is being used for an indication that was not originally thought of when the drug or device was presented for approval. In their article "FDA, Off-Label Use, and Informed Consent: Debunking Myths and Misconceptions" Beck and Azari state the following: The notion that off-label use is itself a "risk" is one of two common misperceptions addressed in this article. The second is that all off-label treatment is *ipso facto* "investigational" or "experimental." It is an accepted principle that once FDA determines that a drug or device can be marketed, a physician's discretionary use of that product (the practice of medicine) is not restricted to the uses indicated on FDA-regulated labels. Off-label use is widespread in the medical community and often is essential to giving patients optimal medical care, both of which medical ethics, FDA, and most courts recognize. Even so, the public (and an occasional court) mistakenly presumes that all off-label treatment is investigational or experimental. " *(Beck, James and Elizabeth Azari. "FDA, Off-Label Use, and Informed Consent: Debunking Myths and Misconceptions." Food and Drug Law Journal, 53 (1998): 71 – 104.)*

The term investigational only applies when a new drug or device has been submitted for approval or when a manufacturer wants to market an approved drug or device for an off-label use. The FDA regulates the marketing of approved drugs and devices but not the prescribing of those drugs or devices. Furthermore the Food and Drug law Journal states the following:
"Off-label uses of medical devices and drugs perform an important therapeutic role in many, if not most, areas of medical practice. Prescriptions for off-label uses of drug products "may account for more than 25% of the approximately 1.6 billion prescriptions written each year, with some recent estimates running as high as 60%." Pediatric uses also are mostly off-label. Thus,
"in some cases, if you didn't use the drug in the off-label way, you'd be guilty of malpractice."*(Beck, p. 80)*

HBOT for brain injuries is simply the off-label use of a FDA approved drug and device. HBOT for brain injuries is clearly an acceptable off-label use. Not only is it an acceptable off-label use but HBOT for brain injuries is a reimbursable diagnosis covered by many state Medicaid plans and Medical Insurance plans. Clearly there is no policy that forbids HBOT for brain-injuries to be a reimbursable diagnosis.

The Medicaid Law for Children and HBOT

Currently, Medicaid reimbursement for hyperbaric oxygen for pediatric brain-injury is "governed" by the 15 indications as "approved" by Centers for Medicare & Medicaid Services (CMS) for the Medicare plan.

Thus, most state Medicaid agencies have decided their reimbursement policies for HBOT should be modeled after Medicare policy, but the Medicare policy on HBOT was devised and created for use by people aged 65 and older as part of their retirement benefits.

How can a Medicaid HBOT policy for children truly provide services for children if its plan is based on a government model that was not designed for children but was designed instead for elderly adults aged 65 and older?

Remember, over 80% of everything prescribed for children are prescribed off-label, and for brain-injured children that number is closer to 100%.

This means the government model for children's healthcare should be that model which will most-include the occurrence of off-label treatments and/or services. This was the exact purpose of the Medicaid Law as discovered by the Georgia father of a cerebral palsy child, Mr. David Freels when he read Paragraph 5 of the EPSDT statute:

> *so children would not be denied treatments and/or services that are "necessary to correct or ameliorate" their physical or mental illnesses or defects "whether the treatment is covered by the state plan or not."*

CMS has two lists on HBOT reimbursement for Medicare recipients: one is termed a "covered" uses list; the second is a "non-covered" uses list.

The "covered" uses list

For purposes of coverage under Medicare, hyperbaric oxygen (HBO) therapy is a modality in which the entire body is exposed to oxygen under increased atmospheric pressure.

A. Covered Conditions.--Program reimbursement for HBO therapy will be limited to that which is administered in a chamber (including the one person unit) and is limited to the following conditions:

1. Acute carbon monoxide intoxication.
2. Decompression illness.
3. Gas embolism.
4. Gas gangrene.
5. Acute traumatic peripheral ischemia. HBO therapy is a valuable adjunctive treatment to be used in combination with accepted standard therapeutic measures when loss of function, limb, or life is threatened.
6. Crush injuries and suturing of severed limbs. As in the previous conditions, HBO therapy would be an adjunctive treatment when loss of function, limb, or life is threatened.
7. Progressive necrotizing infections (necrotizing fasciitis).
8. Acute peripheral arterial insufficiency.
9. Preparation and preservation of compromised skin grafts.
10. Chronic refractory osteomyelitis, unresponsive to conventional medical and surgical management.
11. Osteoradionecrosis as an adjunct to conventional treatment.
12. Soft tissue radionecrosis as an adjunct to conventional treatment.
13. Cyanide poisoning.
14. Actinomycosis, only as an adjunct to conventional therapy when the disease process is refractory to antibiotics and surgical treatment.
15. Diabetic Wounds (Wagner grade 3&4)

No other drug has a "non-covered" list. So, why does HBO have one?

The "non-covered" uses list:

1. Cutaneous, decubitus, and stasis ulcers.
2. Chronic peripheral vascular insufficiency.
3. Anaerobic septicemia and infection other than clostridial.
4. Skin burns (thermal).
5. Senility.
6. Myocardial infarction.
7. Cardiogenic shock.

8. Sickle cell anemia.
9. Acute thermal and chemical pulmonary damage, i.e., smoke inhalation with pulmonary insufficiency.
10. Acute or chronic cerebral vascular insufficiency.
11. Hepatic necrosis.
12. Aerobic septicemia.
13. Nonvascular causes of chronic brain syndrome (Pick's disease, Alzheimer's disease, Korsakoff's disease).
14. Tetanus.
15. Systemic aerobic infection.
16. Organ transplantation.
17. Organ storage.
18. Pulmonary emphysema.
19. Exceptional blood loss anemia.
20. Multiple Sclerosis.
21. Arthritic Diseases.
22. Acute cerebral edema.

Many of these indications are for conditions that afflict many elderly people: bedsores (#1), senility (#5), heart attack/heart condition (#6, #7), stroke--cerebral vascular insufficiency (#10), Alzheimer's (#13), organ transplant (#16, #17), blood loss (#19), arthritis (#21), etc.

It makes no financial sense whatsoever for a Medicaid healthcare plan for children to use a Medicare model on which to base health care decisions for children, particularly brain-injured children.

On November 19, 2002, in the Court of Appeals of Georgia, the Presiding Judge, P.J. Ruffin ruled in favor of a five-year-old child with cerebral palsy by the name of James Freels. Freels' parents had to take Georgia Medicaid to court in order to get reimbursed for HBOT.

The Court said that while state Medicaid programs are "to be given great weight and deference" when it comes to administering this federal program; "nevertheless, the Department must comply with the applicable federal law, and having chosen to participate in the Medicaid program, the State must provide services required under the program."

"Federal law governing the Medicaid program provides that eligible recipients under the age of 21 are entitled to early and periodic screening, diagnostic, and treatment ('EPSDT') services. Specifically, 42 USC 1396d(r)(5) provides that EPSDT services include: 'Such other necessary health care, diagnostic services, treatment, and other measures…to correct or ameliorate defects and physical and mental illnesses and conditions by the screening services, whether or not such services are covered under the State plan."

"In its final decision, the Department (Georgia Medicaid) noted that it 'reimburses only for services which are **medically necessary** and within accepted professional standards'." "The Department denied Medicaid coverage to Freels because it found that…Petitioner failed to satisfy the requisite burden of proof that HBOT treatments are an acceptable standard of medical practice and has not proven the HBOT is medically necessary for Petitioner."

But the Court of Appeals said, "the federal (*Medicaid*) statute does not require that a treatment also be 'an acceptable standard of medical practice' to be eligible for reimbursement. As the superior court ruled, 'instead of requiring proof that HBOT is the accepted standard medical practice, or that it meets the definition of medical necessity reserved for adult Medicaid recipients, the [Department] should have focused its inquiry on whether HBOT was necessary to **correct or ameliorate** [Freels'] physical condition.' The Department's findings show that the proper legal standard was not used in making its reimbursement determination, and we affirm the superior court's reversal of the Department's decision on this basis."

In other words, the Appeals Court reaffirmed that Paragraph five of the EPSDT circumvents the "medical necessary" barrier applied to adults seeking any given therapy by having its own standard for whether a service is reimbursable, and this standard or requirement is only whether that service is necessary to correct or ameliorate. It is no typographical error that "medically necessary" is not found in Paragraph five. The authors knew it can take decades before a treatment, procedure, drug, or device is finally categorized as "medically necessary," and it should be clear now that there really is no process for that to happen anyway, in fact, what is or isn't a medical necessity is often determined by what seem to be arbitrary and capricious machinations that are neither based in science nor economics.

Summary

Today, neonatologists and pediatricians are willing to vigorously resuscitate almost all newborns that are born before 28 weeks gestational age if they appear viable. Of this group we know that about 25% will have an outcome with a major disability. Another 10% are destined for a life of total dependency and an additional 30%-50% will have cognitive, perceptual and behavior problems severe enough to interfere with school performance. According to the Centers for Disease Control (CDC) the average cost of a child with cerebral palsy per year is over half a million dollars with a lifetime cost of $40 million (CDC: Economic costs of Birth Defects and Cerebral Palsy, United States–1992. MMWR 1995: 44;47,695 [see figure #1]). So, the combined savings to the government and the economy of returning function to a child with cerebral palsy are almost im-measurable, but the improved quality of life cannot always be quantified. After all, what is the price of a CP child being able to feed themselves or walk?

If we are willing to resuscitate these children knowing the odds and knowing the cost then why are we so unwilling to accept a treatment that is safe under the right conditions and which seems to benefit some patients and their families with improvements in function and decreased burden of care? The answer is multifaceted, but oxygen is not a patentable drug; therefore, there is not a well funded pharmaceutical marketing campaign behind it. Add to that fact that the principles of hyperbaric or oxygen saturation medicine are not taught in medical school for similar reasons, and most physicians have no exposure to it at all during their training. Do you know what physicians say when you approach them and tell them all the things HBOT can do and has been doing all these years? They say if this were true they would already know about it or point to (non) evidence based reports/assessments that continue to ignore the truth. Having the perfect Randomized, Double Blinded, Controlled (cross-over designed) trial is sought after by medical technocrats as if it were the Holy Grail. Four decades ago the National Academy of Sciences called for a different benchmark when it came to hyperbaric medicine:

"In some [patients], changes in manifestations or course of disease may be such as to permit each patient to serve as his own control. In any situation where application of appropriate measurements gives concrete evidence of changes induced by treatment, the significance of limited numbers of patients is increased"

--from page 13 of a 1963 white paper issued by the US National Academy of Science-National Research Council entitled: "Hyperbaric Oxygenation: Potentialities and Problems".

Children like Augusta, children who have strong documentation showing how hyperbaric oxygenation has changed the clinical course of their illness are being denied this therapy by third party payers and technocrats. Medicaid law, the science of HBOT, and prudent economics are all present behind this therapy, and it is time for it to be made known and available to all brain injured children as Congress originally intended when Medicaid was first created – even if it takes another act of Congress.

Thank you.

Kenneth P. Stoller, M.D.

1. Astrup J, Siesjo BK, Symon L. Thresholds in cerebral ischemia - the ischemic penumbra. Stroke 1981;12:723-25.
2. Rutherford MA. MRI of the neonatal brain. WB Saunders London 2002.
3. Finkel E Stem cells in brain have regenerative potential. Lancet 1996;347:751.
4. Waalkes P, Fitzpatrick DT, Stankus S, Topolski R. Adjunctive HBO treatment of children with cerebral anoxic injury. US Army Med Dept Journal 2001;April-June:13-21.
5. Collett J-M, Vanasse M, Marois P, Amar M, Goldberg J, Lambert J, Lassonde M, Hardy P, Fortin J, Tremblay SD, Montgomery D, Lacroix J, Robinson A, Maijnemar A and the HBO-CP Research Group. Hyperbaric oxygen for children with cerebral palsy: a randomised multicentre trial. Lancet 2001;357:582-6.
6. Marois P et al (2003) Hyperbaric oxygen therapy and cerebral palsy. Dev Med Child Neurol 45:646+
7. Trahan J et al (1999) Changes in Gross Motor Function Measure in children with different types of cerebral palsy. Pediatric Physical Therapy 11:12-17
8. Neubauer RA et al (1990): Enhancing "idling" neurons. Lancet 335:542.
9. Neubauer RA et al (1992): Identification of hypometabolic areas in the brain using brain imaging and hyperbaric oxygen. Clin Nucl Med 1992;17(6):477-481.
10. Neubauer RA (1990). Severe natural gas poisoning successfully treated with hyperbaric oxygen—2 years later. Presented in Prague, Yugoslavia, Proceedings of the 5th International Congress on Neurotoxicology and Occupational Neurology, Sept 24-7, 1990, page 10.
11. Harch PG et al: HMPAO spect brain imaging of acute CO Poisoning and delayed neuropsychological sequelae (DNSS). Undersea & Hyperbaric Medicine, 1994;21(Suppl):15.
12. Harch PG et al: The effect of HBOT tailing treatment on neurological residual and SPECT brain images in type II(cerebral) DCI/CAGE. Undersea & Hyperbaric Medicine, 1994;21(Suppl):30.
13. Harch PG et al: HMPAO SPECT brain imaging and low pressure HBOT in the diagnosis and treatment of chronic traumatic, ischemic, hypoxic and anoxic encephalopathies. Undersea & Hyperbaric Medicine, 1994; 21(Suppl):30.
14. Collins MW, Lovell MR, Mckeag DB. Current Issues in Managing Sports-Related Concussion. JAMA, 1999; 282:2283.
15. Collins MW, Grindel SH, Lovell, MR, et al. Relationship between Concussion and Neuropsychological Performance in College Football Players. JAMA, 1999; 282:964.

Mr. BURTON. MUMS. How did you come up with that?

Ms. GORDON. One of the children in our group when we were discussing it came up with it.

Mr. BURTON. So you came up with the word MUMS. Then you added the words to it.

Ms. GORDON. Right.

Mr. BURTON. Well, you did a good job. Ms. Gordon.

Ms. GORDON. I want to thank you for allowing me to testify and represent the parents of this Nation that have discovered what hyperbaric oxygen can do for their children who have autism and brain damage.

When my daughter Jessica was born 30 years ago, she suffered brain damage from a loss of blood. We were both hemorrhaging through the umbilical cord, and she was born dead and resuscitated, and we were both given ice-cold blood.

In those days, babies like Jessica went to institutions and not home. In fact, the Federal law allowing them to even go to school wouldn't be passed for 2 more years. So we had a lot of battles ahead of us, and today is another battle that I am fighting for children like Jessica and for babies yet to be born so that they won't have to go through what our family went through and that we continue to go through.

I had to give up my teaching career. I had a set of twins and then got divorced. The girls and I were forced to go on SSI, welfare, food stamps, Medicare. It was very stressful and degrading to have two college degrees and to be forced to accept Government help.

So disabilities in the families are not only emotionally but financially devastating to our children and the whole family and the Government.

I realize now that all of this could have been prevented with a little over $3 worth of oxygen. Loss of blood is one of the non-approved conditions for treatment for Hyperbaric Oxygen Therapy. I strongly believe now if Jessica had gotten the therapy immediately, she would have gone home a normal baby.

Instead, I was sent home with a seizuring, spastic, screaming infant with no referral for any therapy or any support. Twenty-five years ago, I started a support group in order to network with other parents whose children also had disabilities. The group has since changed the name of MUMS to the National Parent-to-Parent Network, because we have a lot of fathers involved, and we wanted to include them in our name.

We became international. We now have 19,300 members from 54 countries. Through a newsletter from England, I read about Linda Scotson, whose 14-year-old son was blind and deaf and in a wheelchair, and she had treated him with Hyperbaric Oxygen Therapy, and that he was walking, talking, and was so coordinated that he could ride a two-wheel bike with no hands.

So I was pretty skeptical. But I called Linda. And she told me that he she had a hyperbaric chamber in her living room; she was treating other children. And later on, I found out that there were 500 children in England getting treated that had brain injury, and they were improving.

And the chambers they were using were 100 chambers that—clinics that were set up to treat muscular—multiple sclerosis for free, through a charitable trust. And they would allow children with brain damage to get treated for a nominal fee. Once I shared this information in my newsletter about hyperbarics, more and more parents started wanting information.

Two of my members went with their 8- and 10-year-old daughters out to Florida and got—only 14 treatments is all they could afford. Their daughters improved so much when they came back, one of them raised money and has a chamber in her home. And the other one, her husband used a propane tank and tried to make a chamber. I knew then how desperate parents were and what an impact finally having a hope for improvement in their child's brain damage would do.

Once it was published in the newsletter, it really started a parents' worldwide movement to get hyperbaric covered for children. Stories poured in, articles, MUMS found—one of our MUMS went to—Claudine Nadeau from Quebec—brought her twin sons to Canada. And when she came back with them, Dr. Marois, who was their physiatrist, pediatric physiatrist, was so impressed with their improvements that they both approached the McGill University and got a study where 25 children only received 20 treatments, but they all improved.

Then a group of parents in Quebec formed, and they demanded and put pressure on the government that they do another study. I am just trying to point out that the information is out there, that parents are demanding this, and that there is no way to stop us.

We will go to England and Canada. And what is frightening is some of the parents are talking about, on the listserve, going to the bottom of swimming pools with scuba gear and treating with 100 percent oxygen.

We have had a lot of parents whose children have autism, that the children have totally turned around. My own daughter, who was functioning at a 5-year-old level, she was 25 when I got her treatments. And you could say anything in front of her. I had a friend call me, and she said, "Julie, what did you do to Jessica?" and I said, "What do you mean?"

And she said, "Well, last year, I went to her program, and I asked her a question three times. And she finally pointed to yes." She said, "This year, I went, she drove up to me in her power chair, and asked me how my dog was." This is the different Jessica. Sorry. But the stories are pouring in.

And dramatic stories like Kevin Fickle who was 18-months-old, it was shortly after a vaccine, he got meningitis, went in a coma, five strokes to the brain, all organs shutting down. And his—Dr. Hernandez luckily knew about hyperbarics, but couldn't put him in the chamber until a sore developed, so he could justify treating a wound.

Kevin, today, is now normal. All he has is a slight speech impediment that probably would have been prevented if he had gotten treatment right away. Doctors call me and admit they are sneaking the children in the chamber. One doctor told me that his 51-year-old friend had a viral encephalopathy, and he was brain dead. All of the tests showed he should be removed from life support. And he tried hyperbarics, and he said he walked out of the hospital on his own accord, not well.

And I said, "Why aren't you screaming this from the rooftops?" And he said, "I would lose my job." So this is what medicine has come to. The doctors know it works, but they are not allowed to talk about it or use it.

We have a child we brought today that, I think, she is wanting to be heard from. Shannon called me, and Gracie was on—they, again, wanted to unplug Gracie. But she said—she had called me crying, saying, "I can't let my baby die." And I told her about hyperbarics. She took her by ambulance to Florida. And this little girl is blind, in a coma, all of the other children, this is a rare mitochondrial condition, Cytochrome-C-Reductase Disorder. The doctor said, "There are only five in the world. They are all dead by 2. Let her go. And Shannon, you want to bring her up."

And her mitochondrial disease has gone. There are 40 mitochondrial diseases. My point is, we don't know what will work for us. But this little girl is the oldest living child with this condition. And she keeps getting better with all of the treatments.

So I just want to say one final thing, that I think after the testimony you heard today, if you have a loved one that incurs brain damage, you will be looking for the closest chamber, too. Thank you.

[The prepared statement of Ms. Gordon follows:]

Prepared for the Committee on Government Reform for the May 6th, 2004 Hearing
"Autism Spectrum Disorders: An Update of Federal Government Initiatives and Revolutionary New Treatment of Neurodevelopmental Diseases"

Julie J. Gordon.
150 Custer Court
Green Bay, WI 54301-1243
920-336-5333
www.netnet.net/mums/

Founder & Director of MUMS National Parent-To-Parent Network
Founding Member and Board member of The International Hyperbaric Medical Association
Parent of a 30 year old daughter with Cerebral Palsy & Autism

Before the
Committee on Government Reform
United States House of Representatives

May 6, 2004

CONGRESSIONAL TESTIMONY OF JULIE J. GORDON

Dear Chairman Burton and distinguished members of the Committee, thank you for allowing me to testify and represent the parents of this nation who want to share with you the remarkable results of Hyperbaric Oxygen Therapy for their children with Autism and brain damage.

When my daughter, Jessica, was born in 1973 her brain was damaged from loss of blood during delivery through a slit in the umbilical cord. She was born dead, resuscitated and given ice cold blood transfusions as was I. As her damaged brain swelled the seizures began. In those days babies like Jessica went to institutions, not home with their parents. In spite of the resistance from hospital staff, I chose to take her home. The Federal Law would not be passed for another two years even allowing a child like Jessica into the school system. We had many battles ahead of us and today I am fighting for the babies yet to be born so that they and their families are spared what we had to endure and are still enduring.

I gave up my teaching career to care for her. When she was four years old I gave birth to healthy, gifted twin girls. Divorce is much higher in families with children with disabilities and only the strong marriages survive. Mine did not. The girls and I were forced to go on SSI, welfare, food stamps and Medicaid. It was frustrating and degrading to have two college degrees and to be living below the poverty level and accepting government help with no alternatives. Disabilities in a family are devastating not only emotionally, but financially which in turn makes more people dependent on the government.

This all could have been prevented for our family for just $3. 58 an hour's worth of oxygen. Loss of blood is one of the non-approved conditions for treatment with Hyperbaric Oxygen Therapy (HBO). I strongly believe now that if she had been treated with HBO immediately, she may have gone home perfectly normal. Instead I was sent home with a seizuring, spastic, screaming infant with no referral for any therapy or for any support.

In 1979, when Jessica was six years old and the twins were two, I started a small support group for parents whose children had disabilities. We shared our hopes and sorrows and most of all we supported each other and knew we were no longer alone. We discovered we had power too. When a mother, Donna, with a two year old son who was blind and needed leg surgery called us because the hospital wouldn't let parents stay overnight, we met with the hospital administration and had the policy changed. She slept on a cot in her son's room that night. We grew in strength and number. New mothers knew nothing about the services we did, so a newsletter "*MUMS Matchmaker*" was developed to get information out to those who couldn't attend meetings. Thousands of parents now had a voice to share their emotions, problems and helpful solutions. Milwaukee Children's hospital reestablished the Parent Rooms on each floor because of our editorial complaint in the MUMS newsletter.

As parents of children with rare disorders joined, we established a matching service to link them with each other. Because of the uniqueness of this service, over the years MUMS grew to be international and now has over 19,300 members from 54 countries covering 3400 diagnoses. Over two thousand Professionals joined and refer parents to us for help.

In 1995, through the exchange of newsletters from England, I discovered that 500 children with Cerebral Palsy in England were being treated with HBO and were improving. One article told about Linda Scotson's 16 year-old son who went from being blind, deaf and in a wheelchair; to seeing, hearing and riding a two-wheel bike no handed. This seemed to me to be impossible so I called Linda in England and she said she had a large chamber in her living room in which she treated him and other children and verified their improvements.

After receiving more HBO information anonymously about people coming out of comas and "Idling neurons" becoming active in the brain using HBO, I decided to share this information with my Medical Board of Advisors and five parents to see what they thought. My Pediatric Neurosurgeon and two parents, Laurel & Diane, went to investigate Dr. Neubauer's clinic in Florida where he was treating off-label conditions. The parents each got 14 treatments for their daughters and saw amazing improvements. They were so excited when they returned that Laurel raised money and put a chamber in her home and Diane's husband tried to build one out of a propane tank.

Their experiences made me decided to publish an article about Hyperbaric Oxygen in our MUMS newsletter in 1997 and the response was an amazement to even me. You see when your child has brain damage the doctors tell you there is nothing that can be done. Hyperbaric Oxygen Therapy gave us hope - our only hope.

Naive parents willing to pay cash started knocking on the doors of hospitals with chambers only to be turned away. We were shocked! Parents in the Military on bases with huge multi-placed chambers were also turned away. Parents sent MUMS articles they found about HBOT and we developed a packet of information and started distributing it. Parents started going to England and Canada for treatments and shared their experiences – more information for our HBO packet. With the increased demand for HBOT from parents, existing free-standing wound care clinics and new clinics started to treat our children. Parents and grandparents whose children had improved opened clinics.

As parents reported back to MUMS of the existence of these HBO clinics we started a list of clinics to share with interested parents. MUMS became the clearinghouse for parents to find clinics and for clinics to get listed if they were willing to treat off-label. Parents from all over the world started contacting MUMS and sharing their experiences – the first to be treated in Germany and Malaysia and France. A group of parents in South Africa bought a chamber and were treating their children and shared their testimonials. Presently we have 131 HBO free standing clinics listed that will treat off-label conditions. In addition in England there are 100 clinics and 11 in Scotland treating Multiple Sclerosis for free through a charitable trust and they have opened their doors to children with brain damage for a small fee.

A letter to the editor in Exceptional Parent Magazine from two parents requested more information on HBOT. I wrote and the response with MUMS' address and phone numbers was published in the magazine so more parents called and letters poured in. The letter I had responded to turned out to be from Claudine Nadeau from Quebec and Debbie Nardone from Illinois. Debbie was a member of MUMS and met Claudine through the Internet. Debbie shared the information she had from the MUMS newsletter and the two of them decided to meet with their sons in England to get HBOT.

When Claudine brought her twin sons, Michel and Matheau, back from England, Dr. Marois, their pediatric physiatrist, was amazed at their improvements. Claudine and he approached McGill University in Quebec to do a study. As a result, the McGill Pilot Study took place Oct 15 – Dec. 15, 1998 in Montreal. The results were amazing considering the 25 children ages 3 to 8 years old with spastic diplegia Cerebral Palsy only got 20 treatments at 1.75 atmospheres. Results showed reduction in spasticity in hip adductors, hamstrings and ankle plantar flexors. Patellar tendon and Achilles tendon reflexes were found to be significantly reduced. It was reported that there was significant improvement in the children for walking and sitting as well as for knee walking. The study concluded that HBO improves function in children with spastic diplegia, Cerebral Palsy.

Following the results of this study, a group of parents from Quebec, spearheaded by Annie Lachaud, organized a Parent Movement to further research on HBOT. Because of the pressure put on the Canadian government by these parents, 1.2 million dollars was allocated for another McGill study which included 111 children at three different locations. The study was completed in August 1999.

As Dr. Paul Harch has stated, "The real story behind the McGill Pilot Trial is not the findings of the study, it is the story of a group of mothers organized and connected by the MUMS Network and Internet who became a force so powerful that they were able to overcome tremendous resistance and accomplish what a group of physicians were unable to achieve in over 50 years."

Because of the studies and requests from Canadian parents more clinics opened in Canada. In 1999 a new HBO clinic with a 10 person multiplace chamber was opening in Coquitlam, British Columbia and offered me free treatments for Jessica when they called to get on our HBO clinic list. I had never really thought about getting her treatments because I couldn't afford them and I truly felt at age 25 years old it was too late. But how could I turn down this wonderful opportunity? Parents had shared the names of organizations that provide free airline travel to children for medical purposes and I contacted one and we were approved. Amy, a friend from Palm Springs flew with her 11 year-old son, Ari, who has severe Cerebral Palsy and Autism also and the four of us shared a hotel room. Our children each got 40 treatments with a protocol of 1.75 ata twice a day. We know now this was a dangerous protocol because 1.5 ata is safer and more effective, but we were all experimenting with our children and we followed the protocol used in England. During his second treatment, Ari's tight arm easily could be raised above his head. His speech became clearer and his legs more relaxed and his Autistic behaviors lessened.

The noticeable changes in Jessica occurred after about the 20th HBO treatment. Her muscle tone became much more loose especially when she was in a relaxed state. Her posture in her wheelchair became straighter and her head control much better. She used both her hands together much more. She even lifted a towel off her tray with both hands to wipe her mouth off. She used to slide off the bench in the chamber, but now with her relaxed legs she could sit with ease and with only slight assistance from me.
Her alertness and attention span increased. One technician noticed she seemed "more animated". She enjoyed having me read books to her which she never had the attention span to enjoy before. The sentences she spelled out on her communication board were more complicated as are the words and phrases and ideas she uses. She initiates conversations now instead of needing prompting.

Prior to HBO Jessica could only make the "M" sound and say "Mama". Jessica has started to talk and can now say 5 words including saying her sister's name, "Abbie". She can say "Hi" and delights in hearing the new sounds come out of her mouth. Overall she just seems smarter and more alert and happier.

Jessica was evaluated at Central Center in Madison, Wisconsin before and after her Hyperbaric Oxygen Treatments. Previous evaluations showed her getting more spastic. When stood Jessica's legs scissored (crossed severely)and she was up on her toes. After 61 HBO treatments her physical therapy report says, "Significant changes (+/-) in the following: hip extension (10° to -15° right) and (5° to -10° left), hip internal rotation (35° to 50° right and 35° to 55° left), left shoulder abduction (135° to 145°) and her right wrist extension (55° to 65°). Jessica also had an improvement in her hamstring flexibility on the left as evidenced by improved straight leg raises (45° to 55°). When placed in quadruped (on all fours), Jessica was able to weight bear on both hands with hands open. She was able to accept the weight more evenly on all four extremities and even began to weight shift back and forth with assistance. She had attempts at moving her legs and also advancing her left arm. During her previous admission (before HBO), Jessica had difficulty keeping the weight back over her hips and kept her hands more fisted and required maximal assistance so this was an improvement. Movement into tall kneeling also improved." Her improvements were documented! Now when I stand her, her legs are apart and her feet are flat on the floor. I only need to hold the back of her head for support. A recent report said her ankle flexibility improved 20%.

In the Coquitlam clinic there were 30 children a day getting treatments. I met two children who had been seizuring all day long and both completely stopped with HBOT even though the parents had taken them off all medications. A seven year-old Canadian boy, Brett could walk, but had such low tone in his hands he could not even hold a crayon. After HBOT, his favorite thing to do was to color. A five year old French Canadian girl walked alone for the first time in the waiting room as we all applauded. Nineteen year old Adam from Texas not only got more relaxed and responsive, but his severe psoriasis almost disappeared! Two year old, Mitch, who was a shaken baby from Minnesota scooted off his blanket for the first time since his injury and stopped seizuring totally.

In July 1999, Dr. Neubauer, a pioneer in treating off-label with HBO, had *The First Symposium On Hyperbarics and The Brain Injured Child* in Florida and parents came from all over. This gathering fueled our excitement. Listservs started and parents shared their children's improvements and others joined wanting to know more. At the symposium we met a man, Tom Fox, from Alabama who ran a free-standing Hyperbaric Wound Care clinic and he was so touched by what he saw, he offered five of us free treatments if we would come to Alabama. To his surprise a few weeks later we were all on his doorstep.

While there I told Tom if he could bring a mobile chamber to Wisconsin, I would help him find interested parents to bring their children for treatments. For fear of having the FDA stop us, we parked the unit on an Indian Reservation outside of Green Bay. Because so many parents in Wisconsin were interested in HBOT we had no trouble finding willing parents. Billy's mother drove 1 ½ hours one way to get the treatments. Billy has a Chromosome 9;11 Balanced Translocation and is Autistic and had very crossed eyes. His mother, Lynette said because of his sensory issues, he would never wear a hood and she had trouble getting him to go in the chamber for the first treatment. After one treatment, Billy's eyes straightened and after seven treatments they were permanently straight. He became so much calmer and loved crawling in the chamber. Billy would try and put his own hood on even before we were at pressure.

Another man from Oklahoma, Mike, bought a mobile chamber because he had a niece with Cerebral Palsy and a sister who had a stroke. He also brought his chamber to Wisconsin. Now Jessica and many more children in Wisconsin were able to get HBOT on a regular basis without having to travel.

Jessica to date has had a total of 215 treatments and she is a totally different child. Another MUM, Sherri, who brings her son's companion dog once a year to demonstrate at Jessica's adult program called me and asked what I had done to Jessica. I asked her why. She said, "Well last year I saw Jessica and asked her a question three times before she answered by pointing to "yes". This year she drove up to me in her powerchair and asked how my dog was. This demonstrates the new Jessica. The most profound change in her is the lessening of her autistic behaviors. Her thought patterns are more mature and complex. She wishes she could get married and that she would like to "try" and drive a car. She initiates conversation, is so aware of her surroundings we have to be careful what we say in front of her, where before she was in her own little world.

Her father wanted to make her a CD of music and I told him she never indicated an interest in music, but I would ask her. She spelled out, "Walking on Broken Glass", Sit Down, You're Rocking The Boat" and "Uptown Girl" I was astonished! She listens to her music CDs all the time which is more age appropriate.
She can problem solve now. Recently she spelled out she wished we had an elevator so she could go down in the basement. Her sister just moved out into an upstairs apartment and when I told her I cannot show her the apartment because of the stairs, she asked me to make a video of it for her to see. She likes to watch "Sex In The City" (how normal do I want her to be? :>}) and reminds me a few minutes before 8 o'clock every night to turn on "Larry King Live". She never even watched TV before HBOT. She tells me when she has a headache, is sick or if her tray is dirty. She even laughed and called me stupid!

Another new development which prior to HBOT she was unable to do is that Jessica has a job making personalized stationery and envelopes and brings home a paycheck ! She never had the interest or ability before. Throughout her years of schooling a constant goal that was never reached was for her to tell me what went on in school. Now she voluntarily tells me she went to the museum, or that they had "Take Your Daughters To Work Day". Her communication and social skills are becoming near normal thanks to HBOT. Although she has been G-tube fed for the last ten years she is eating more by mouth and even eats corn-on-the-cob without difficulty.

Every parent fears for the future and worries who will take care of their child when they no longer can. With Jessica's new awareness and communication skills I feel more confident she will be able to communicate her needs and will better be able to fend for herself when I am gone. It is so amazing how the brain can improve after 25 years with Oxygen and a little pressure.

I have gathered 100s of cases but I will present just a few, but please read the other documentation I have brought for your review:

- In 1998 a five year old little boy in Texas, Edgar Gonzalez, who was hit by a car and had a traumatic brain injury was in a coma for three weeks with a score of "7" on the Glasgow coma scale. A hyperbaric doctor in Galveston, Sally Robinson, tried Hyperbaric Oxygen treatments on him and he is now back to normal except for a lumbering gait when he walks! One of our MUMS in the Galveston study triggered by the success with Edgar told us her daughter's vision went from cortically blind to 20/20.

- Shortly after his daughter Rebecca's complicated birth and cardiac arrest for 35 minutes, Ed Nemeth of Sacramento, California and his wife were presented with the unspeakable, yet strongly suggested single choice for their first-born child: discontinue life support or allow their child to continue brain dead. Devoid of options the Nemeth's discontinued life support; Rebecca rallied and lived. Five years later through their indefatigable efforts the Nemeths found HBOT and after a short course of HBOT their daughter experienced a quantum leap in neuro-cognitive function and significantly improved movement and coordination. Ed is now involved with two hyperbaric clinics and funded the Second First Symposium On Hyperbarics and The Brain Injured Child in Florida because of his interest in furthering HBOT for children like his Rebecca.

➤ Shannon Kentiz of Wisconsin called me crying that her two year old daughter, Gracie who had Cytochrome-C-Reductase Disorder and was on life support. This is a very rare mitochondrial condition (there are 40 types) that destroys the brain and the doctors told her the five children they knew about all died by the age of 2 years. They were pressuring Shannon to remove the life support and she said she could not watch her baby die. Shannon was given no options. I explained to her that no one had tried Hyperbaric Oxygen Therapy on Mitochondrial Disorders, but maybe it was worth a try. Since she had nothing to lose, she brought her daughter to Florida by ambulance. Gracie was lethargic and blind and in a coma. After hyperbarics she is walking, pulling the pens out of her doctor's pockets and can see. Her mitochondrial disease is totally gone and they now think with more HBO she will be normal. I spoke with her ophthomoligist in Madison who was so amazed he is doing a study using HBO for visual problems. Carlos Ponte, Gracie's pediatrician was so impressed he has changed his career direction, has moved from Wisconsin to Florida and is studying to be the medical director of a Hyperbaric clinic there.

➤ Michelle Divino from Illinois has two children with Autism. Her son age 9 years was somewhat verbal before treatments, but echolalic (repeating what others said only), had obsessive behavior with self-stimulating behaviors as a norm. He would typically play obsessive games to amuse himself, screaming to vocalize his needs, and only used nouns to communicate. After 40 HBOT he properly uses pronouns, is using prepositions, conjunctions, and will repeat his sentences over and over until he is satisfied with how they sound. He has shown real emotion, and even told a lie! He is now able to tell what is wrong when he is upset. He says "good night" spontaneously. Once he said "Look at that green car, it's beautiful". without any prompting at all and said he a certain game he was playing. Her daughter is 2 and a half, nonverbal, and somewhat aloof showing very little interest in her mother before treatment, preferring her father. Her daily routine consisted of watching videos all day and "reading" her magazines and books. After the first few treatments her daughter said, "bye-bye" and "mama" and began to began to seek out her mother to play. She showed more interest in her siblings as well. Her interest in videos slowed down and she began playing in the sandbox which was taboo before HBOT. She began to run (which she was unable to do before HBOT) and attempted stairs one foot over the other versus one stair at a time. Overall she became more aware, less aloof and will look at her mother and smile when she says hello 2 out of 10 times versus not at all.
http://www.netnet.net/mums/AutismHBO.htm

➤ One of our fathers whose son had a near-drowning episode while he was visiting his sister in California knew about Hyperbaric Oxygen Therapy before the incident. He told me he literally got down on his knees, crying and begging the doctors at Loma Linda to treat his son. They refused.

➤ Debbie, a MUM in Wisconsin, was pregnant with twins, and had her leg amputated because of flesh-eating bacteria. When this failed to stop the spread of the bacteria she was given HBOT which totally killed the bacteria. Why was HBOT not the treatment of choice before amputation? The twins were 24 weeks premature and both have Cerebral Palsy. Her other child has Achondroplasia dwarfism.

➤ I called a doctor that I heard from parents was treating children with Cerebral Palsy-sneaking them in the chamber. He told me he would treat children with brain injuries, but that I should not publish it. He said he was seeing the same improvements in the children that was documented in the MUMS' newsletters. He then told me that he had a 51 year old friend who had suffered a viral encephalopathy and had been in a coma for five weeks. All the tests they did on him, MRI, EEG, showed no brain function and that he was clinically dead. The ventilator was removed but he did not die. He told the family that before they made the final decision to stop feeding him, he wanted to put him in the chamber. After the Hyperbaric Oxygen Treatments his friend walked out of the hospital, not well, but of his own accord!! I asked him why he wasn't shouting this from the rooftops? He told me he would lose his job for treating off-label. What state is our medical system in that our government allocates millions of dollars for research each year, yet doctors are afraid to come forward with the truth about HBOT for fear of retribution?

➢ David Freels of Georgia has a 10 year old son Jimmy who has Cerebral Palsy. HBOT improved Jimmy tremendously so David asked his state Medicaid to pay for the treatments. When they refused he sued and won. He based his claim on the language of the EPSDT statue that states in paragraph (5) 139d(r) that States provide "such other necessary health care...treatment and other measures...to correct or ameliorate defects and physical and mental illnesses and conditions discovered by the screening services, whether or not such services are covered under the State plan." The state has appealed.

Ga. Dept't of Cmty. Health v. Freels, 576 S. E. 2d (Ct. App. 2002). Held that the EPSDT statute required only that a treatment be necessary to correct or ameliorate physical or mental conditions, not that a treatment be an acceptable standard of medical practice.

➢ Finally I present you with the story of Kevin Fickle who I consider the poster child for Hyperbaric Oxygen therapy. Kevin Fickle of Slidell, Louisiana was 11 months old when a viral encephalopathy put him in a coma. He was on life support, had five infarcts to his brain and all his organs were shutting down. His doctor knew about HBO, but because of the off-label ban on using it for brain damage he had to wait until Kevin developed the typical meningitis sore on the back of his head eleven days later. This was the ticket he needed to justify use of the chamber for wound healing. After three treatments Kevin fought the ventilator and after ten he was crawling around the chamber. His parents are members of MUMS and update me with pictures periodically. The only side effect he still has is a speech delay otherwise he is a normal boy. If he had been able to be treated earlier his speech would probably not have been affected.
His story was featured on Lifetime's Beyond Chance with Melissa Etheridge.
http://www.musa.org/Stories/kevin_fickle.htm

I get calls almost daily from parents with questions about HBOT. They cannot ask their doctors who have no training in this field. Dr. Harch, who is on the MUMS' Medical Advisory Board has been kind and dedicated enough to respond to many of them personally. He and I cannot keep up with the demand and there needs to be a better system for dissemination of information. Without studies we do not have the answers. We can only guess from our experiences and those of others.

With our nation in an economic crisis we cannot afford to ignore the possibility of HBOT reducing not only the medical costs, but the excruciating, life-altering pain and suffering

experienced by so many. The parent movement has taken on a life of its own. Desperate parents are going to continue to get HBOT for their children no matter what you decide today. Some are even talking about treating their children with scuba gear and 100% oxygen at the bottom of their swimming pools. We are crawling into chambers in the back of semis hidden on Indian reservations and in warehouses and having chambers installed in our homes. Parents are second mortgaging their homes and taking out huge unrepayable loans. Nothing can stop parents from getting HBOT for their children, but you can help us make it safe and available. We need studies to determine the safest and most efficatious protocol.
The question is not whether Hyperbaric Oxygen Therapy works. The exciting question is what other conditions will Hyperbaric improve or cure.

With your help, the testimony you have heard today could help revolutionize the medical industry and put hyperbaric oxygen as a treatment of first choice rather than a last resort. Infants born with severe brain damage could be sent home as normal babies. People involved in accidents suffering from traumatic brain injuries and those who have strokes could have the damage to their brains reversed or eliminated if treated immediately.

You know in your heart, after what you have heard today, if a loved one of yours incurred brain damage you would be desperately looking for the closest hyperbaric chamber too.

Thank you so much for your valuable time.

Julie Gordon

Mr. BURTON. Well, thank you, Ms. Gordon. I really appreciate what MUMS are doing and the information you have given us.

Dr. Weldon, who is with us, he has to leave. If you don't mind.

Ms. WATSON. No.

Mr. BURTON. I would like for him, since he is a physician—he is very interested in the mercury aspects of autism and all these other things. He can be a big help to us in communicating with our health agencies.

So, Dr. Weldon, do you have some questions or comments?

Mr. WELDON. Yes, I do, Mr. Chairman. And thank you for inviting me. It is great to be back. I miss the committee. Though I must admit, you worked me pretty hard when I was on the committee.

I certainly thank the ranking member as well for giving me the opportunity to be here.

Mr. WELDON. Dr. Buttar, you used DMPS as your chelation agent?

Dr. BUTTAR. Yes, I have been using DMPS for about 8 years intravenously and about 2 years in transdermal form.

Mr. WELDON. You have to forgive me, I got called out when you were beginning your testimony. I thought I saw one of your slides that talked about administering an oral chelating agent as well. Is that correct?

Dr. BUTTAR. DMPS was developed in Russia. It had actually been used in Europe for 50 years. Its method, primary method of application is actually oral dosing.

The problems are that, first, it is 50 percent absorbed, 50 to 55 percent absorbed through the gastrointestinal mucosa.

The second problem is in the children that we treated with the DMPS orally; within 5 to 7 days they started having abdominal cramping and pain.

And third, this patient population, as most of the patient population that I deal with, have already altered gut function. They have basically chronic GI distress, GI dysbiosis, many other types of digestive problems and absorption problems.

And so these children were not getting better with the oral version. That is when we went to the transdermal. We had actually used the transdermal previously in adults but found it not to be as efficacious as the IV, because IVs are done every other week. And the transdermal was not yielding as much mercury as the IV version.

Mr. WELDON. And tell me about your transdermal application. How do you do that? What is the technology involved there?

Dr. BUTTAR. It is—DMPS——

Mr. WELDON. Is it a commercially available product?

Dr. BUTTAR. No, sir. DMPS is not approved in the United States. Its sister product, which is DMSA, which is made by the same manufacturer out of Germany, is approved but happens to be a neurotoxin.

DMPS is something that has, for some strange reason, the only way it was approved—let me take that back. It was—it has been approved for bulk compounding pharmacy usage, but that was only for 3 years. And now, strangely enough, since 2001, we can't find any information from the FDA. FDA is right now pushing for compounding pharmacies——

Mr. WELDON. The question I really had is, do you just apply it to the skin and put an adhesive bandage on it?

Dr. BUTTAR. No. Actually it is—I should have brought some with me, and my son would have demonstrated how to use it. But it is drops. DMPS is highly oxygen reactive, so it has to be stabilized. Once we stabilize it, we conjugate it with certain amino acids, including Glutathione, and then—it is a lotion, essentially.

Mr. WELDON. A lotion?

Dr. BUTTAR. A lotion. It is dosed at 1.5 milligrams per kilogram. It is drops, 1 milligram per drop. And a child just takes it themselves. It is dosed every other day, because it is very effective at pulling out mercury and arsenic, but it is not selective. It pulls out essential minerals.

Mr. WELDON. You used the transdermal, though. Are you applying it to the skin?

Dr. BUTTAR. That's correct.

Mr. WELDON. So the children just rub it on their skin?

Dr. BUTTAR. That's correct. To the volar aspect of the forearm, to the latissimus area, anywhere that has a high vascular supply.

Mr. WELDON. In bathing, the mercury is withdrawn, or they absorb it into their body, and it comes out in the urine?

Dr. BUTTAR. Actually, what our study showed was that we—we measured it actually increasing your hair yield, fecal as well as urine. So it is hepatically—it may even be hepatically treated, but it is basically—primarily the body excretes mercury through the biliary system. But we have seen it being excreted through the renal system as well as through the hair.

Mr. WELDON. Dr. Harch, are you on the faculty at the University of Oklahoma? Did I hear you say that?

Dr. HARCH. No. I am not. LSU, New Orleans. I am on the faculty there.

Mr. WELDON. You are on the faculty at LSU?

Dr. HARCH. I am working with the Oklahoma School of Medicine.

Mr. WELDON. OK. Have you published any of the studies that support the claims that you made in your testimony?

Dr. HARCH. Some. It has plainly been in book chapters. There have been some isolated articles as well. And we have an animal model now that we are doing the final preparation for manuscript for.

Mr. WELDON. A lot of the resistance on the part of insurers and third-party payers is the failure to develop an adequate body of knowledge published in the peer-reviewed literature supporting the claims and assertions regarding the applications of Hyperbaric Oxygen Therapy.

And is your professional association moving to develop the documentation necessary to obtain wider acceptance within the medical profession of Hyperbaric Oxygen Therapy? Because I have seen people have come to my office and shown me these case reports that are very, very dramatic. And it would seem to me that you should be able to publish some of this information.

Dr. HARCH. The answer is yes. We are trying to disseminate that information.

The other answer is that a surprising amount of this information is available and previously published. And I will just give you an example.

In 1992, the Journal of Neurosurgery of Rockswold, 168 patients, randomized prospective controlled trial of hyperbaric oxygen in acute severe traumatic brain injury, highly significant reduction in mortality, 60 percent reduction in mortality in the hyperbaric oxygen group.

They have another study that is now showing a similar type of effect. But this is an irrefutable study. The problem was, even though it is the same outcome used by the certifying bodies for reimbursement of hyperbaric oxygen, they did not have patients—a greater number in the hyperbaric group—in the high outcome group.

The fact that is lost on them is that they saved 60 percent of these people. If we compare this to American Heart Association Cardiac Arrest, for instance, they have such dismal outcomes, and they are just looking for any degree of survival.

There is actually a followup study that was published 2 years ago, Journal of Neurosurgery, same group, Rockswold. They went back and did the same severe traumatic brain injury group, or equivalent, and did elegant metabolic studies. And what they showed was a single hyperbaric treatment could recouple brain bloodflow and metabolism in an injured brain.

Never been demonstrated in the history of science. It is out there. And unfortunately, it hasn't been appreciated or picked up. It is a political issue, partly, in medicine. I can discuss it with you. But——

Mr. WELDON. Well, actually I am——

Mr. BURTON. Before you leave, I would like to know, real briefly, why you say it is a political issue. I would like for him to elaborate real quickly.

Dr. HARCH. Well, basically it is—I am going to be real blunt about this. There has been a group of doctors who have controlled the supply of information on Hyperbaric Oxygen Therapy through a medical society. And there has been an intense hatred by one of them, an ex-president, for the man who originally developed some of this information, Dr. Neubauer.

And with this institutionalization and the destruction of his reputation, the science of what he says has been thrown out and, for years, everything associated with it. And that, in a nutshell, is why this has been stunted in its application and dissemination. It has been at a medical society level. It is a personal doctor issue. And I can verify that.

Mr. WELDON. I was just going to add, for the record, one of my partners when I practiced medicine was certified in hyperbarics. And sometimes, he would take the weekend off, so I would pick up his cases. And so I had to learn a little bit about it. And I have seen some significant outcomes from its application.

Mr. Chairman, I have to go. Thank you very much for indulging me.

Mr. BURTON. Thank you.

Mr. WELDON. Also, thank the ranking member.

Mr. BURTON. As you leave, though, we will be drafting some letters with questions to the HHS people. We would like to have you as a signatory to the letters to try to find out their reasons.

Mr. WELDON. I would be very happy to support you in that.

Ms. WATSON. May I, before Dr. Weldon leaves. Mr. Chairman, I just want to comment before you leave, Doctor.

I would hope that we would send a very strong letter to be able to locate the research and the findings and publicize it, because it goes beyond a political problem. It goes to depriving those who could benefit from this discovery.

My experience with hyperbaric chambers was down in Micronesia when we had people diving too deep and drownings and so on. But this is the first that I heard that brain injuries, and I guess it makes sense, get oxygen to the brain, maybe heart problems and so on, could be affected by the hyperbaric chambers.

And so I just wanted to say that before you left so you will join with us in very strong support on releasing the research.

Mr. WELDON. I would be glad to do that. Thank you.

Dr. HARCH. Congressman Watson, can I respond?

Mr. BURTON. I am going to yield to Ms. Watson now, and you can respond to her as Dr. Weldon leaves, and she can ask any questions.

Dr. HARCH. The actual other issue for Dr. Weldon is that there has been a failure by the medical community of hyperbaric medicine to adequately explain what is going on with hyperbaric oxygen. And what is happening in chronic wounding is that the intermittent exposure to oxygen is causing growth of new tissue.

You cannot have that unless you go through the DNA of the cell to then begin to transcribe new proteins, growth factors, etc. In the last 6 years now, elegant and molecular biochemical experiments have been done showing that hyperbaric oxygen signals the DNA to begin the transcription of sequences that code for growth hormones, growth receptors and so on.

And that is the secret behind what has happened with Shannon Kentiz' daughter, Gracie. In a mitochondria disorder thought to be DNA-linked, hyperbaric oxygen is signaling and affecting the DNA and effecting a permanent change in this child. That is the underlying basis of hyperbaric oxygen.

Dr. BUTTAR. Excuse me.

Before Dr. Weldon leaves, Congressman Burton, is it all right for this 5-year-old, who, at the age of 3, was not speaking at all, to address the chairman and the respective Members of Congress that are here?

Mr. BURTON. Only if he doesn't challenge me to a chess match.

Master ABID BUTTAR. Mr. Burton and Ms. Watson and Dr. Weldon, thank you for helping my dad getting all people better and children better.

Ms. WATSON. I just want to say, this is kind of like a miracle that we are hearing.

And thank you so much, Dr. Buttar, for bringing him.

And Abid, thank you so much for speaking to us. And you did that very well.

Master ABID BUTTAR. Thanks.

Ms. WATSON. I just want to say, the politics of medicine is as rigorous as the politics that we are into. We are going through the same thing in another area of medicine with dentistry and the filling and mercury fillings, amalgam. And we have the American Dental Association against us. And we had the California Association as well.

And I authored legislation over 14 years ago now, to just inform parents of the risks and the benefits. And we don't have a piece out that is what I would consider practical, informative and truthful. And that is because it is cheaper to put the amalgams in.

But in terms of hyperbaric chambers and hyperbaric medication, what would be the cost of a struggling family? And I heard $30,000 somewhere, I guess for a specific case. But can the ordinary, average family afford this treatment?

Dr. HARCH. Well, you might want to ask the families that. They go through considerable sacrifice to get this, because they often have to travel at distances, because the hospital-based physicians where these chambers are located have been threatened by the medical society for treating something that is not on this list, that is only partially supported by science.

Mr. BURTON. Is that the AMA you are talking about?

Dr. HARCH. Oh, no, it is not. It is the Undersea and Hyperbaric Medical Society.

Mr. BURTON. OK.

Dr. HARCH. And so what has happened is, the cost of this has now been shifted to outpatient freestanding centers where, if in a doctor-attended facility, you are able to access this, you pay $150 to $200 a treatment. At centers that are run by parents, other individuals, groups that have gotten together, it is $50 or $100 a treatment, even. People have even used portable chambers. They now are putting them in their homes and delivering the treatment very cheaply.

So the actual cost of the treatment is not substantial, compared to the hospital billing for this. The hospitals are charging, combined doctor and hospital fee, up to $1,400 per hour. It is prohibitive. It is a disgrace. And it is unnecessary.

Ms. WATSON. Is this to try to force you not to use that procedure?

Dr. HARCH. No.

Ms. WATSON. What is the cost——

Dr. HARCH. To maximize reimbursement. It is gouging. It is not cost.

Dr. BUTTAR. If I may, Congresslady Watson, if I may address this also. It is a similar reason that chelation therapy intravenously is considered to be a part of alternative medicine, if you will. Yet every emergency room in every city in our country, the only method that is approved by the FDA of removing acute lead for lead toxicity is EDTA infusion.

They charge $980 for an infusion in the hospital. But if you add a couple of minerals to it and some vitamins to it and you do it in the doctor's outpatient office, then it is called chelation therapy, although it is only $150.

Same treatment, less constituents within the treatment, and it is called a different treatment. And it is not reimbursable. Again, it is a money issue, just like Dr. Harch said.

Ms. WATSON. I am trying to understand. I heard somewhere along the way that it took just one treatment. Was that for an infant?

Dr. HARCH. No, it is for adults. I said I have treated approximately 400 patients. Over half of them are adults.

Part of the problem is also this is an off-label, off-FDA-label use of hyperbaric oxygen, at least for a number of the neurological applications. And that is one of the other reasons that it has been difficult to get in the hospitals.

Ms. WATSON. Where are these chambers located? Are they located throughout the country? Is it a regional approach that is taken with hospitals in using one site?

Dr. HARCH. No. No. They are spread throughout the country. There are approximately 600 facilities now that are hospital-based.

And due to recent changes in Medicare reimbursement, two things: One was the approval of treatment of diabetic foot wounds, which we had a very large part in getting approved.

And the second is a doubling of the hospital-based reimbursement for this. Hyperbaric facilities are now being put in hospitals all around the country. Additionally, hyperbaric chambers are being put in freestanding facilities. And to my knowledge now, there are maybe 130 of those.

So there are over 700. The numbers that are increasing are substantial.

One for-profit company that I know of, there are probably—I am going to say 8 or 10 large ones, putting a new facility in a hospital approximately every, oh, 2 to 3 weeks. So we are seeing a substantial increase in installation of chambers, which will translate into increased usage, but not necessarily for these more devastating neurologic problems.

Ms. WATSON. I am not clear on the coverage. Would Medicaid cover it?

Dr. HARCH. That is a big fight right now. Medicaid has two tracks. One is medical necessity. And one is necessity to—or not necessity, but to ameliorate or correct problems with disabled children.

And it is under that that Hyperbaric Oxygen Therapy likely will be reimbursable. Unfortunately, it is in the courts right now.

Ms. WATSON. Medical necessity?

Dr. HARCH. No, no, no. On this statute, amelioration or correction.

Ms. WATSON. Is medical necessity coverable?

Dr. HARCH. Tricky. It is on this other list of FDA indications, many of which do not have any remunerative science that there is behind the treatment of cerebral palsy with hyperbaric oxygen.

But again, I am going to go to politics. It was approved by a group of doctors, some who had a very personal interest because that was their pet subject. And in fact, it got approved. Once approved, it was adopted by the FDA, adopted somewhat by Medicare, third party insurers, and Medicaid.

So what has happened is, the Medicaid reimbursement for these things is not necessarily tied to science. And one of the indications which had the greatest science for we don't have reimbursement for.

Ms. WATSON. Well, I am hoping that this committee can be instrumental in gathering the scientific evidence, the empirical evidence and making it public through HHS or through one of our agencies. I think it is an absolute necessity that we do that.

And I think it might require, Mr. Chair, some additional legislation to be sure that this treatment is recognized and covered under one of our programs. And I don't know exactly—we would have to kind of research where it should be.

Because to see the results that I see in this room, convince me that we have a void there, and we have to let a lot of children and adults just languish out there when they could be affected very positively and their health could improve.

Dr. HARCH. Thank you. We were praying that you would get into this.

Mr. BURTON. Well, your prayers have been answered.

You know, you don't need to do that. Do we have anybody in here from the Food and Drug Administration or HHS? I didn't think so.

What we will do, though, is we will need as much documentation, and we need it, if you will, in as much as possible layman's language so that we understand it. And we can also put it in the kind of question format that they will understand and that they will know that we know, so that they have to respond. If I send a bunch of hyperbole over there that they know Congressman Burton is not a doctor and Dr. Watson is not a medical doctor, they might be able to, you know, give us the shuffle off to Buffalo.

But if it is in layman's language and we ask questions that are readily understood, then they will have to respond in like kind. And I know that Dr. Weldon, who does have the knowledge to be of great assistance, and Dr. Watson and I will be very happy to pursue this.

But we need the facts. We need the documentation, too, but we need the facts so that we can write an intelligent letter that they will have to respond to.

Beyond that, regarding legislation, Dr. Watson, Congresswoman Watson, how many titles do you have? We will see what we can do legislatively to put some heat on our health agencies as well. But we need to have all of the knowledge we can from you guys.

Ms. Gordon, thank you very much for working so hard on MUMS. I am sorry that you and your daughter had such a tough time.

I appreciate you, doctors, and all of the hard work that you are doing.

And thank you to all of the people in the audience who came. I have met some of you before.

This fight regarding autism is one that has been going on for a long time. We have been able to get mercury out of all of the children's vaccines but three. They are still in adult vaccines. But you know, Congresswoman Watson, Weldon, myself we are going to be around here for a while. We will just keep pushing until we get the whole enchilada.

Anyhow, thank you very much. We stand adjourned.

[Whereupon, at 4:25 p.m., the subcommittee was adjourned.]

[The prepared statement of Hon. Ileana Ros-Lehtinen and additional information submitted for the hearing record follow:]

The Honorable Ileana Ros-Lehtinen
Statement for Autism Hearing
May 6, 2004

I am truly inspired by the tireless dedication of those who are working to find a cure for autism. Thank you to all who are joining us today for this important briefing.

I would like to especially thank Chairman Burton for holding this very significant hearing today to discuss an issue of great importance to all, that of Autism Spectrum Disorders. Chairman Burton is a true friend to all who are affected by Autism and we are grateful for his valiant leadership. Thank you, Dan.

I look forward to hearing from our esteemed guests who have labored over the issue of finding a cure for autism. Your work in the field of this disorder demonstrates the symbiotic relationship that the government holds with the community. Thank you for coming today.

My dearest friends, Charles Flick and Patience Plumer Flick have two precious children with Autism. I have watched with great admiration as Bonnie and Willis have grown and developed into bright and vivacious young people. They are a gift to all who know them. I am inspired by the tireless dedication of families like the Flicks who sacrifice tremendously for the good of their children. It is a great blessing to see the tremendous love which strengthens the familial bonds and their desire to preserve the dignity and promote the independence of each and every individual.

I am blessed to have them in my life and am committed to working with my colleagues to make sure that a cure is found for Autism.

Incidents of autism have become increasingly prevalent in today's society. Current estimates are that 1.5 million Americans are diagnosed with either autism or an autism spectrum disorder (ASD). The epidemic is hitting the nation hard. California alone saw a doubling of reported cases during the four years between1998 to 2002.

It is critical that we work together to find a cure for autism. It is vital that the autism community has a voice and access to the most advanced medical resources. As a Member of the Congressional Autism Caucus, I am firmly committed to ensuring that a cure is found for those afflicted. Increased federal funding for NIH research into autism increased from about $10.5 million in FY 1995 to $99 million to FY 2005 (estimate). CDC commitment jumped from less than $300,000 in 1995 to $12.5 million in FY 04.

The United States government has begun to acknowledge the present and future public health implications of the autism epidemic by establishing an Interagency Autism Coordinating Committee. In addition, it is working to investigate revolutionary treatments that have been shown to improve the medical condition of children afflicted with autism.

It is exciting to note that, HHS and the Department of Education sponsored the first-ever "National Autism Summit" in November 2003, to further address the concerns of the autism community. This summit was essential to bridging the relationship between the government, non-governmental organizations, and private citizens.

A lot of the attention has been given regarding the link between mercury and autism, with mercury being the possible factor underlying the etiology of this condition.

While much progress has been made in the area of research, there is still a great deal more that needs to be done to help our precious autistic children and adults. We must continue to together to help find a cure for autism. I will continue to work together with my colleagues in Congress for all who are affected by Autism.

Thank you to everyone, once again, for your exceptional contribution to the enhancement of the lives of all those affected by autism. You are dynamic and energetic champions for the cause of our community, and I wish you much continued success.

Thank you, Mr. Chairman.

Statement for the Record
Before the Subcommittee on Wellness and Human Rights
Committee on Government Reform
United States House of Representatives

Autism Spectrum Disorders: An Update of Agency Initiatives and Revolutionary New Treatment of Neurodevelopmental Diseases

Statement of the U.S. Department of Health and Human Services

For Release on Delivery
Expected at 2:00 PM
on May 6, 2004

The Department of Health and Human Services (HHS) is pleased to submit a statement for the record with respect to the Autism Summit Conference of November 2003 and progress made by the National Institutes of Health (NIH) and other member organizations of the Interagency Autism Coordinating Committee (IACC) since that meeting. Section 104 of the Children's Health Act of 2000, Public Law 106-310, authorized the establishment of an interagency autism coordinating committee to coordinate research and other efforts with regard to autism within the HHS. Secretary Tommy Thompson delegated the authority to establish the IACC to the NIH in April 2001. The National Institute of Mental Health (NIMH) at the NIH was designated the lead for this activity.

HHS agencies represented include the following: the NIH Autism Coordinating Committee (ACC) members [NIMH, the National Institute of Child Health and Human Development (NICHD), the National Institute on Deafness and Other Communication Disorders (NIDCD), the National Institute of Environmental Health Sciences (NIEHS), and the National Institute of Neurological Disorders and Stroke (NINDS)], the Health Resources and Services Administration (HRSA), the Centers for Disease Control and Prevention (CDC), the Agency for Toxic Substances and Disease Registry (ATSDR), the Substance Abuse and Mental Health Services Administration (SAMHSA), the Administration for Children and Families (ACF), the Food and Drug Administration (FDA), the Centers for Medicare and Medicaid Services (CMS), and the Agency for Healthcare Research and Quality (AHRQ), as well as the Department of Education (ED) (specifically, the Office of Special Education and Rehabilitative Services).

This statement includes information about the Autism Research Matrix, which was presented and discussed at the Autism Summit Conference. Additional information about the Autism Research Matrix can be obtained from two reports recently submitted to Congress: Congressional Appropriations Committee Report on the State of Autism Research (found at: http://www.nimh.nih.gov/autismiacc/CongApprCommRep.pdf); and the December 2003 submission of the Annual Report to Congress on Autism, required by the Children's Health Act of 2000 (found at: http://www.nimh.nih.gov/autismiacc/autismreport2004.pdf).

IACC Autism Research Matrix

The Conference Report on the Consolidated Appropriations Bill for FY 2003, which included the appropriations for the Departments of Labor, Health and Human Services and Education and related agencies, (Conference Report No.108-10), requested that the IACC "convene a panel of outstanding scientists to assess the field of autism research, and identify roadblocks that may be hindering progress in understanding its causes and best treatment options." The final product was to be the development of a research matrix focusing on the causes and best treatment options for autism that includes opportunities for voluntary and private funding organizations. In response to this request, the IACC convened a panel of science experts in July 2003 to document both roadblocks to understanding causes and best treatment options for autism, as well as goals and activities to overcome these roadblocks. A list of roadblocks was created, and the autism research matrix was designed to include goals and activities for the next 10 years. The goals and activities generally fall within the following categories: characterization of autism (i.e., phenotype), screening, early intervention, school and community interventions, specific treatments, neuroscience, and epidemiology. As requested by the conferees, the matrix will be a living document, subject to ongoing revision. It will be periodically revisited and revised based on achievement of some of the goals, as well as on new knowledge and insights.

Autism Summit Conference

In order to expand on the work of the IACC, HHS and ED co-sponsored the Autism Summit Conference on November 19 and 20, 2003, in Washington, DC. This national conference focused on the Federal government's role in biomedical autism research, early screening and diagnosis, and improving access to autism services. The summit provided a public forum to disseminate, evaluate and integrate the latest practice and science-based autism information among Federal, academic, and community participants.

A major goal of the summit was to develop an information exchange among the autism community, experts in specific areas, and Federal agencies that advance autism research and services. Another goal was to foster partnerships among these groups. As part of the summit's emphasis on increasing communication and collaboration between government and the private sector, several public/private partnerships created to enhance research in needed areas were presented. These new partnerships included initiatives for data and software sharing, public and private collaboration for an awareness campaign, and joint ventures to encourage research with populations at high-risk for autism, as well as genetic research.

The summit was segmented into three themes that represent areas most urgently needing attention. The first theme, the integration of autism services throughout the lifespan, included issues for those living with autism, such as fragmented services provided by educational and other systems. The second major theme, implementing autism screening and diagnosis, included presentations on existing screening instruments and implementation of screening practices in the community. Relevant research and current clinical practices were discussed. The third theme was biomedical research. In this component, programs were discussed that built on the work of the expert panel of scientists created by congressional request to develop the Autism Research Matrix to identify and advance high-priority research goals. Federal officials, researchers, and community members discussed such topics as genetics, epidemiology, and early intervention. In addition, the Director of NIMH presented on the overall Autism Research Matrix, to receive public input before final approval by the IACC.

Interagency Autism Coordinating Committee Meetings

At the November 21, 2003, IACC meeting, the IACC approved the current version of the Autism Research Matrix. The IACC intends to evaluate progress on a yearly basis and will begin discussion of implementation at its upcoming meeting on May 11, 2004, for which further information is found at: http://www.nimh.nih.gov/autismiacc/events.cfm. The NIH-ACC members (NIMH, NICHD, NIDCD, NIEHS, and NINDS) are assuming primary responsibility for implementation, such as documenting in-progress activities and developing initiatives, including the types of private and partnership activities referred to in the conference language requesting the matrix and discussed at the Autism Summit. Over the past few years, NIH has considerably expanded its autism research portfolio and enhanced its coordination of autism research. NIH support of autism research grew from $22 million in FY 1997 to $93 million in FY 2003, with estimated increases to $96 million in FY 2004 and $99 million in the FY 2005 President's Budget request. NIH supports autism research in the areas of genetics, neurobiology, early diagnosis, services, and treatment, while the CDC has expanded its efforts in supporting research on the epidemiology of autism.

Specifically, CDC's autism budget has grown significantly in the past few years. During FYs 1995-1999, the annual appropriated amount for CDC autism activities was less than $1 million. In FY 2000, that figure increased to just over $1 million and for FY 2004 is estimated at about $16 million. Special studies on the causes of autism are ongoing at six sites through the five CDC-funded Centers for Autism and Developmental Disabilities Research and Epidemiology, and the sites have joined forces to design a collaborative case-control study to identify risk factors and causes of autism. CDC's autism surveillance efforts are also proceeding, which will provide data needed to characterize autism spectrum disorders, determine rates of autism, and identify trends. In addition, CDC's Autism Awareness Campaign has moved forward. Since November, the Campaign has received feedback reinforcing the importance of engaging physicians and other health care professionals early on. Recently, through and agreement with CDC, the American Academy of Pediatrics distributed an "Autism A.L.A.R.M." to the Nation's pediatricians, encouraging them to screen children early and refer those who may have autism for further evaluation or services. To further engage pediatricians and other health care professionals as critical players in an effort to help children with autism develop and reach their full potential, CDC will be disseminating additional materials to this audience in the coming days. These activities provide a framework for allowing investigators to study important questions about autism.

The state of autism research has advanced substantially in the past year with the increased infrastructure that has permitted expansion of research into the causes and best treatment options for autism. For instance, NIH has now funded a total of eight centers under the Studies to Advance Autism Research and Treatment (STAART) Centers Program http://www.nimh.nih.gov/autismiacc/staartcenters.cfm. These centers complement the 10 Collaborative Programs of Excellence in Autism (CPEA) Centers Network, and two Children's Environmental Health Research Centers that focus on autism. These network activities are in addtion to the increased numbers of individual grants being funded to support autism research.

The NIH-ACC also is developing new initiatives and priorities intended to implement Matrix activities and achieve Matrix goals. For example, on April 2, 2004, the NIH-ACC reissued a program announcement to potential grant applicants entitled, "Research on Autism and Autism Spectrum Disorders," which may be found at: http://grants.nih.gov/grants/guide/pa-files/PA-04-085.html. Other major initiatives that advance Matrix goals include: expansion of a repository at the NIMH Center for Genetic

Studies, which establishes resources for genetic studies and enhances data sharing; two NIH sponsored workshops on confronting methodological challenges in research on interventions; and the establishment of the National Autism Brain Bank, which creates infrastructure for enhanced brain acquisition for neuropathological investigations to characterize the morphological aspects of the pathophysiology of autism.

In addition to these NIH activities, other HHS agencies such as the CDC and FDA are contributing substantially to progress on the IACC Research Matrix. For instance, the CDC is partnering with several private organizations to launch an Autism Awareness Campaign, entitled: "Learn the Signs/Act Early." CDC efforts are also allowing for substantial progress on collecting rigorous epidemiological data, with activities such as the Centers for Autism and Developmental Disabilities Research and Epidemiology (CADDRE) and the Autism and Developmental Disabilities Monitoring Network (ADDM Net).

As FDA stated in its December 2002 testimony before the Committee on Government Reform, the FDA's Center for Biologics Evaluation and Research (CBER) is conducting a follow-up study of reports of autism following vaccination to the Vaccine Adverse Event Reporting System (VAERS). As part of the study, CBER is reviewing available medical records and surveying parents and others who have reported autism after vaccinations. The results of this portion of the study might be used to help improve the government's ability to communicate the risks and benefits of vaccination to the public. Although this study will not be able to determine whether vaccination causes autism, it might result in the generation of hypotheses that could be evaluated in subsequent controlled epidemiological studies.

Implementation of the Matrix is also occurring through the IACC's established subcommittees on autism screening and the organization of autism treatment services. Both subcommittees are now working to coordinate activities among IACC members and with the relevant stakeholders in the medical and services communities. Additional discussion regarding the implementation of the Matrix will take place at the May 11 meeting of the IACC.

Summary

In sum, the Department of Health and Human Services, through the IACC as well as public-private partnerships, is expanding its efforts as a result of the Autism Summit Conference and IACC Autism Research Matrix. These activities will continue to be monitored and evaluated on a yearly basis by the IACC, and reflected in changes made to the Matrix as progress occurs.

Windsor L. & Pamela C. Anderson
134 Hogan Lane N.E.
Warren, Ohio 44484
(330) 856-1032
wla7@neo.rr.com

May 5, 2004

The Honorable Tim Ryan
U.S. House of Representatives
222 Cannon HOB
Washington, DC 20515

Dear Congressman Ryan:

We are the grandparents of Charles who happens to have autism. Charles is five years old, lives in Huntersville, North Carolina with his parents and two younger sisters, and was diagnosed with autism at the age of three. Charles' parents, Kim and Rob Anderson, have endured fear, pain, guilt, violence, humiliation, anger, desperation, frustration, futility, and financial hardship. They have been treated with condescension, patronized, and threatened with a future of doom. One pediatrician told them Charles was below-normal intelligence and, perhaps slightly retarded. At times, Charles behavior is uncontrollable and at five his vocabulary is limited. Kim and Rob have endured this and more in their quest to help Charles out of his autistic shell. Along the way, they used and paid numerous professionals for help, received all kinds of advice, some good and some bad. They followed programs, medical advice and diets. Again some advice was good and some bad. The financial cost of all of this has been devastating, with costs in 2003 alone exceeding $75,000. Can you imagine the horror of a young family facing this?

There is a good, loving, helpless child trapped inside this bizarre behavior of Charles' autism. Kim and Rob have been determined to get him out. The process of educating and reaching Charles is time-consuming and expensive. There are many victories and celebrations and some disappointments and regrets. Their goal is for Charles to be in a mainstream education beginning with the 2006 school year. So far, their behavior modification and educational program is on track. They know that if they give up and let go, Charles will be lost forever.

Kim and Rob discovered that early intervention is the key. The 1987 Lovass study supports the conclusion that when autistic children are given intensive (30-40 hrs per week) Applied Behavior Analysis (ABA) therapy many are successfully mainstreamed with their typically developing peers. Charles has been in a similar program for 2 years, has shown significant progress, and is succeeding with his mainstream goal for the 2006 school year. Without the support and intensive ABA therapy, Charles could very well be facing a future in an institution, being mute, and totally detached from society. With the appropriate funding and education programs in place, autistic children will have a much higher probability of beating the disorder all together and the long-term cost for families and society will be much less.

The heartbreaking disease of autism isn't just about caring for a difficult, challenging child. It also can mean sacrificing the parents and the child's relationships, careers, and financial security. Almost all families face the obstacles of finding and providing affordable medical treatment, therapy services, appropriate education and legal representation for these challenging children. The impact of this disease cannot be overstated, nor can the stress and heartache ever be over-emphasized.

Parents with autistic children do not have millions of dollars of money, paid time off of work to travel to Capitol Hill, and paid lobbyists to support their needs and views. Parents of students with disabilities must work hard to deal with some very difficult and costly life circumstances. They cannot afford to leave their families and jobs. They need an advocate for their children from afar. They need elected officials and their appointees to listen and understand. The problem of autism is simply not going to go away. We cannot afford to leave these children behind by inadequate program funding or by doing nothing.

It will take pages to detail the battles and hostility Kim and Rob faced when they tried to provide Charles with the "free and appropriate" education he is entitled to under law. (Enclosed is the 48-page brief of fact and law submitted on behalf of Charles) And while we want to believe that special education teachers and school administrators are devoted to these vulnerable children, you need only review the brief of this due-process hearing to realize that this is not always the reality. Sometimes, there is resentment and retaliation when school systems are forced to deal with a disability they don't understand or an education they will not provide. The availability of the "free and appropriate" education Charles is entitled to could mean the difference between a rewarding and functional future, or a lifetime of disability requiring almost constant support.

Pam and I are asking your support to make sure children with disabilities will continue to be entitled to a "free and appropriate public education" ('FAPE") measurable on an objective basis and that if the local education agency fails in this mandate, as will sometimes occur, the child will continue to have meaningful "due process" entitlements to challenge the school agency and petition for relief. In this connection, objective and measurable, short-term goals and objectives are imperative. Parent input is an essential ingredient with these goals and with accountability. Education systems must be held accountable for students with disabilities. Charles' due-process hearing brief indicates that the school district failed to develop appropriate goals and objectives and services for Charles' IEP. The school district also failed to measure or track where Charles was functioning on the objectives. Parents of children with disabilities need and are entitled to more accountability than generic reports reciting that Johnny is doing "just fine." If "No Child Left Behind" means anything, we must continue to insist on *objectively* measurable criteria to gauge educational progress (or the lack thereof). We should not be relying on the purely subjective measure of asking the fox to tell us how the chickens in the chicken coop are doing. The answer may be predicable ("the chickens are doing just fine!") but it is not likely to be accurate.

Pam and I were told that another proposal that is floating around concerns attorneys' fees. Someone is proposing a $4,000 cap on attorneys' fees recoveries. First, there is no corresponding limit on what school districts may spend on their counsel. Second, every case is different, and some complicated cases go for quite a few days (Charles' hearing was about 28 days). Third, parents win attorneys' fees ONLY if they win the case via a decision. Please do not support the adoption of such a modification.

We also need your support for IDEA funding. While we would like "full funding" immediately, we believe the more realistic approach is to press for significantly increased IDEA funding. The financial strain placed on our education system is enormous as they attempt to educate these children who have very special needs. The States and local school districts need additional funding to improve special education and programs to ensure "No Child (is) Left Behind".

As your constituent and as grandparents of a child with autism, we respectfully request your support. Our family knows all to well about autism and what it encompasses, Kim and Rob's devotion, and the emotional and financial strain placed on the family. Early intervention and education are crucial for the child's development. Autism is not a disorder of childhood; instead it is a disorder of development. Charles now fights with all his might, to increase his vocabulary. He gets frustrated easily because it is difficult to communicate to the rest of the world his wants, needs or desires. It is heart breaking, to see such a smart little boy, have to fight so hard to become the normal boy we know he can be. He is not alone. There are many children just like him. They need our help. They need your help!

Very truly yours,

Windsor L. Anderson
Pamela C. Anderson

Windsor L. & Pamela C. Anderson

Cc: Congressman Dan Burton
2185 Rayburn HOB
Washington, DC 20515